Praise for *200 Pomegranates and an Audience of One*

"From beginning to end, *200 Pomegranates and an Audience of One* captivated me. Shawn's gift of storytelling, when combined with his passion for artistry, makes for an inspiring read. This is certainly a book I'll be talking about for a while!"
—Anne Jackson, author of *Mad Church Disease* and blogger at FlowerDust.net

"Shawn Wood captures the essence of lives lived before God for the sole purpose of pleasing Him. By serving others, each real-life character in this book demonstrates how humility and sincerity are expressed for His pleasure and for His glory. Amazing insight into how to live a life in the spirit of Christ."
—Billy Hornsby, Association of Related Churches

"I am fortunate enough to rub shoulders with Shawn every day as we pursue ministry together. I have watched as he approaches each area of responsibility he has been given with the eye of an artist toward an audience of one. He lives what he writes about, and our lives and ministries have been better for it. I am confident you will be encouraged and better off for being around Shawn, as I have been, as you connect with God's artistic vision for your life through this book."
—Greg Surratt, Lead Pastor, Seacoast Church

"Shawn's core concept is so fresh and vivid that I find myself thinking about it time and time again. I hope we can get a copy of *200 Pomegranates and an Audience of One* into the hands of every bank executive, auto mechanic, student, stay-at-home mom (everyone!) who wants to live a life of destiny and significance. Get ready for God to add his *extra* to your *ordinary* as Shawn illustrates the beauty and adventure of a life lived for an audience of one."
—Steven Furtick, Pastor, Elevation Church

"Moved. Inspired. Convicted. These are just a few words that come to mind. Shawn Wood has a rare ability to pull nuggets from the Bible while telling stories, and writes as though he were sitting down having a conversation with you. This is a book for anyone who wants to be great at something—parenting, teaching, leading, whatever. God has a purpose for you to be great at something, and this book will give you the motivation and inspiration to get there."

—Tim Stevens, Executive Pastor, Granger Community Church

"I have seen in Shawn, as a friend and coworker, the heart of an artist who sincerely strives for greatness in the eyes of God. In *200 Pomegranates* he shares the often humorous and sometimes heartbreaking experiences from his own life that have shaped that heart."

—Geoff Surratt, Pastor of Ministries, Seacoast Church, and author of *Multi-Site Revolution*

"Excellence honors God. And that's why I love this book. It will not only help stretch your imagination. It will also challenge you to do little things like they are big things."

—Mark Batterson, Lead Pastor, National Community Church

"In *200 Pomegranates and an Audience of One*, Shawn Wood explains how God uses the ordinary to do extraordinary things. With stories of humor, pain, and biblical truth, Shawn illustrates how God can fill our lives with meaning and influence."

—Craig Groeschel, Senior Pastor, LifeChurch.tv and author of *Confessions of a Pastor*

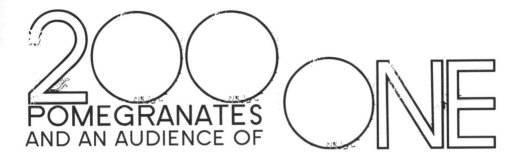

200 POMEGRANATES
AND AN AUDIENCE OF ONE

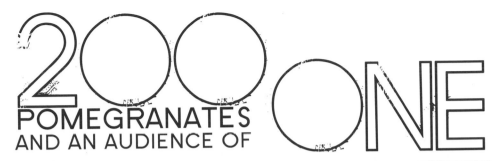

200 POMEGRANATES AND AN AUDIENCE OF ONE

CREATING A LIFE OF MEANING AND INFLUENCE

SHAWN WOOD

Abingdon Press
Nashville

200 POMEGRANATES AND AN AUDIENCE OF ONE
CREATING A LIFE OF MEANING AND INFLUENCE

This book is printed on acid-free paper.

Library of Congress Cataloging-in-Publication Data

Wood, Shawn.
  200 pomegranates and an audience of one : creating a life of meaning and influence / Shawn Wood.
    p. cm.
  ISBN 978-0-687-65492-5 (binding: pbk., adhesive perfect : alk. paper)
  1. Christian life. 2. Self-actualization (Psychology)—Religious aspects—Christianity. 3. Meaning (Philosophy)—Religious aspects—Christianity. 4. Influence (Psychology)—Religious aspects—Christianity. I. Title.

  BV4501.3.W657 2008
  248.4—dc22

                                                                    2008021601

All scripture quotations, unless noted otherwise, are taken from *THE MESSAGE*. Copyright © Eugene H. Peterson, 1993, 1994, 1995, 1996, 2000, 2001, 2002. Used by permission of NavPress Publishing Group.

Scripture quotations marked (NLT) are taken from the *Holy Bible*, New Living Translation, copyright © 1996. Used by permission of Tyndale House Publishers, Inc., Wheaton, Illinois 60189. All rights reserved.

Scripture quotations marked (NCV) are taken from the New Century Version.® Copyright © 2005 by Thomas Nelson, Inc. Used by permission. All rights reserved.

Scripture quotations marked (NIV) are taken from the Holy Bible, NEW INTERNATIONAL VERSION®. Copyright © 1973, 1978, 1984 by International Bible Society. Used by permission of International Bible Society.

08 09 10 11 12 13 14 15 16 17—10 9 8 7 6 5 4 3 2 1

MANUFACTURED IN THE UNITED STATES OF AMERICA

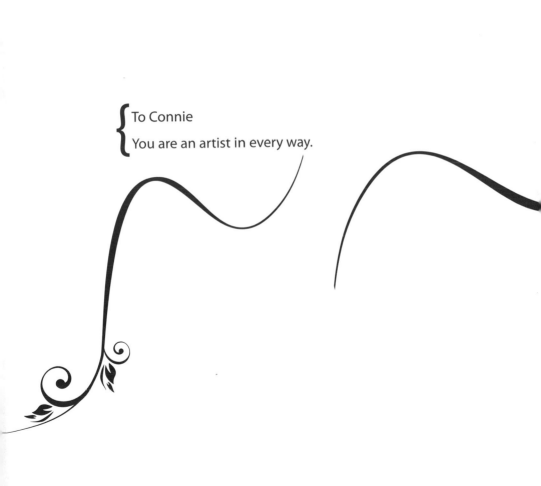

To Connie

You are an artist in every way.

{ *Huram cast two bronze pillars, each 27 feet tall and 18 feet in circumference. For the tops of the pillars he cast bronze capitals, each 7½ feet tall. Each capital was decorated with seven sets of latticework and interwoven chains. . . . The capitals on the two pillars had 200 pomegranates in two rows around them, beside the rounded surface next to the latticework. Huram set the pillars at the entrance of the Temple, one toward the south and one toward the north. . . . And so the work on the pillars was finished.*

I Kings 7:15-17, 20-21, 22b NLT

CONTENTS

ACKNOWLEDGMENTS

This book is a pomegranate to Jesus, who saved me.

To Connie: My high school sweetheart, my best friend, and my wife. Thank you for being a wonderful partner in this beautifully choreographed dance. Almost every single word of this book was typed sitting on the couch beside you. You believed I was an author before I did. I love you.

To my sweetheart, Isabelle: You are a beautiful work of art. Be careful with your finger—I am wrapped around it.

To Mama: We have been through a lot together, grown up together, and now are enjoying life together. Thanks for being willing to make the choice to be a young mom.

To the team of unbelievable servants at Seacoast Church: You are all artists and your masterpiece is the changed lives that we see every weekend. Lori, Ashley, Nate, Marty, and Zach—you are all rock-stars in my opinion and the best team in the world. Thank you to Greg, Geoff, Byron, and Mac. Your leadership and friendship is valued.

This book is in memory of my uncle Herb. You were an artist in everything that you did, and you literally saved the life of this little boy. You left us way too early—but we still marvel at your work, like any great artist's work. I am one piece of work that you helped shape and I will represent you as well as I can.

INTRODUCTION

the artist's mandate

As I watched every deliberate, yet seemingly effortless, movement, I was amazed. Each and every action led to yet another beautiful layer of the canvas that was taking shape. Color and imagination, heart and soul were being poured into every detail of this work before her, and it was at this very moment that I knew I was watching an artist at her work. Her canvas seemed at times to war against her, but with determination she was creating something very special.

The artist was my wife and the canvas my nearly two-year-old daughter. **Mommies are artists.**

The opportunity for a hostile situation stood before him like a huge rock of granite. It seemed almost impossible to move and determined to stay hard and unshaped. But using the power of words my friend Josh has the ability to craft and sculpt beautiful art out of the most callous of situations. With the use of just the right words he creates an art show on display for the world to see.
Coworkers are artists.

Karen has lost her husband of nearly thirty years at the age of fifty-one. As I sit with her in a time of heartache, I realize that just moments earlier she lost more than I can imagine and that she can barely breathe. In coming days we are both struck by the fact that God still has her here for a purpose, but through tear-clouded eyes it seems hard to find. Then she says it—words that will stay with me for some time. Through her grief she reminds herself that she has a group of first graders waiting for her. She is the architect of these little lives and though that may be all that is left, that is a task worth living for. So every day she wakes up because there are lives to be built and dreams to be planned.

Teachers are artists.

Terry leaves no detail untouched. I have seem him take the extra time to look over a job a second or third time to make sure that his work is just right. I have seen him do this when the customer is there, but I happen to know that he does it when no one is looking as well. His job is more than making money to him; his business is more than just a reflection of himself. Every oil change is an opportunity to represent God and an opportunity to build a legacy. Every tune-up is an orchestra he brings into harmony with a wave of his baton.

Mechanics are artists.

No longer is art limited to painters and musicians. Each one of us is an artist, endowed by our Creator with skills and talents that can make our world a more beautiful place. Every good mom is an artist, molding her children as a creation of God. Every teacher makes a mark on the young people in his or her classroom. Every ethical businessperson leaves a legacy of people seeing God through his or her careful and honest work.

Through the story of an obscure but exemplary biblical character, we will explore the value of creative work in God's eyes. Huram of Tyre was an artist in the literal sense—a bronzeworker helping construct the temple in Jerusalem.

My guess is that unless you are an Old Testament scholar you have probably never heard of Huram of Tyre. In fact, a quick search of "Huram, 1 Kings, Bible" on Google and Wikipedia brings up nothing except the stories in 1 Kings and Chronicles that inspired this book.

As I think through every male I have known in my life, I can recollect knowing an Adam, a Joshua, a Joseph, a Noah, and an Abraham. Believe it or not I even once knew a dude named Melchizedek. I have never known a Huram. There are not a lot of parents thinking they have finally landed on a name for their child after studying 1 Kings. If they did, it would probably not even be the Huram this book is about.

Some of the confusion comes with the apparent lack of creativity on the part of Huram's mom. Being from Tyre, she named her son after the king, also named Huram. If you read carefully, you will find that there are two men named Huram from Tyre in 1 Kings, and they are contemporaries. One is a king. The Huram this book focuses on is not the king. Then the confusion gets even thicker as he is called *Huram-abi* in Chronicles, that is, *Huram is my father.* Can we get one more Huram, please?

Several of the modern translations try to make things a little easier by spelling one name Hiram and the other Huram (since the original Hebrew text didn't have vowels in it anyway). It makes me want to sing the "you say tomayto, I say tomahto" song. I love the way *The Message* paraphrase of the Bible tries to clear things up for us a little in a parenthetical explanation in 1 Kings 7:13 (emphasis mine): "King Solomon sent to Tyre and asked Hiram *(not the king; another Hiram)* to come."

So now that we have cleared that up, let me tell you a little about the book you are about to read. Along our quest to discover how to live a meaningful and influential life, we're going to follow the lead of this guy Huram and the work of art he created. It's a very small story of a not-so-famous guy in a book that few have read. How is that for a sales pitch? Let's be honest, there are parts of the book of 1 Kings that have been the bane of many of our "we are going to read the Bible in a year" New Year's resolutions. (Come on, you know you have been tempted to skim parts of 1 Kings too.) First Kings is a basic history of the kings of Israel—thrilling to the history buffs among us, but laborious to those looking for a lot of practical application. However, tucked away in the Old Testament book is the often overlooked story of a man we never knew but whose example can teach us a lot.

Through the story of the two hundred pomegranates that Huram created for an audience of one, we will see how he made an amazing contribution just by using his talents and doing his job with integrity and humility. We will come to understand how we too can create something beautiful in the eyes of God simply by being the best parent, coach, teacher, welder, pastor, accountant, spouse, trash collector, (fill in your position here) that we can be.

In the story of Huram and his two hundred pomegranates we find the artist's mandate—five essential components of life-artistry:

- Get great at something
- Do something with that talent
- Invest yourself in things that will last and that others will benefit from
- Work for an audience of one, because sometimes our best work is seen only by God
- Finish what you start

If everyone is an artist then life itself is a grand work of art.

What are you creating?

get great at something

My wife and I had recently moved to the Raleigh, North Carolina, area for me to work on my master's degree in theology. We were the ripe ages of twenty-one and twenty-two and had been married about ten minutes (OK, five months, but who is counting?) when we drove into the Research Triangle to start our life together.

We had been planning the move for all of our married lives, so in our wisdom we had saved about eighteen dollars as a safety net. Because of our financial shortcomings we needed to get jobs, save some money, and then we would look for a place to rent. In one of the few early wise choices, I had arranged to live rent-free for a month or so with some friends, who were also in the area for school, just to get our feet wet.

Knowing this plan and our situation, just one week after moving to Raleigh I came home with a Polaroid picture of our new home and presented it to my wife in a card I bought from the drugstore. "Look what I bought us today, baby!" I exclaimed. Yes, you read that right. I bought our first home (and our first car) without my wife seeing them. I would later learn that not only is that not nice—it's just stupid.

Fast-forward a month or so and there we were in a house that my wife saw for the first time through a Polaroid, making a life in the big city. Life was good. We were loving the new area. We were loving being married. Connie was even starting to love the house. On a few occasions, however, I had heard her mention that there were a couple of things about the house that she really would like to change. "Hardwood floors would look good," she had commented, and, "French doors opening out to the deck would be nice as well."

We were eight months into this marriage and I was really trying to learn how not to make another Polaroid mistake, so I took note of these comments and thought to myself, "Hardwood floors, that can't be that difficult."

So I set out on the pilgrimage that all men must go on at some time in their young lives: the first trip to Home Depot without their dad. I fumbled through the store looking for what I would need to destroy—I mean, remodel—my home.

Like a five-year-old sheepishly meandering through the aisles of Mr. Wonka's factory, I finally saw the golden ticket. Apparently they had just invented hardwood floors for dummies. These were not like the hardwood floors that they make now that just snap in place with hardly any work at all. I wish those had been around—my two-year-old could put those together like they were Lego toys. You had to nail these in place, but at least they were prefinished, which was a whole lot better than seeing me with a can of varnish. Given my history of only swinging hammers to smash spiders, this was just the deal for me. I quickly guessed at how much I would need to cover our little abode and bought a few boxes of hardwood flooring. As I walked to the front of the store I remembered that there was a football game on that afternoon that I really wanted to watch. I reasoned in my head that surely I could get this done in an hour or two.

As afternoon settled on the Wood home, I had gotten as far as ripping up all of the carpet in our living room. (I had definitely underestimated the time this would take.) Dust was billowing all over the place and I was a seminary student on the verge of cussing out loud. I had already cussed a lot in my head. What I had failed to realize is that hammering nails into hardwood is hard. It is even harder if you try to use a Fisher-Price hammer made for preschoolers. So I loaded up and headed back to mecca. As I entered Home Depot for the second time in one day, I decided to try using my words and found another human who might be able to answer my questions. I have often wondered what this man must have been thinking as I asked him how to install the hardwood floor, which I had already purchased, onto the floor of my home that—thanks to me—had no carpet. He explained that I needed a nail gun. That sounded fun and dangerous all at the same time. "Sweet! Where do I get one?" I asked. Lucky for me they will rent a nail gun to any seven-year-old with his daddy's credit card, and so I was off again to remodel.

Long story even longer, six months later I was still trying to get the hardwoods finished in my home when the opportunity of my young marriage presented itself like a Christmas gift on New Year's Eve. My wife was leaving town for a long weekend at a women's conference. That's when the plan came to me. I would work 24/7 to get the hardwoods completed; and for a big surprise birthday present for my honey, I would install those French doors as well! As soon as she drove out of sight, I jumped in my car and made the now all-too-familiar drive to the Depot where, like an episode of *Cheers,* they really did all know my name. I went in and grabbed the closest thing to French doors I could find (I think they were from the Netherlands or someplace, but hey, we were on a budget) and was off to do some more damage. I had finally found an excuse to buy a sledgehammer, and as soon as I got home I started knocking out sheetrock. As I knocked away more and more sheetrock and more and more two-by-fours that seemed to be in the way of my Dutch doors, I felt this rush of excitement. My wife had only been gone for two hours and look at all of the progress I was making! I had torn down nearly 25 percent of the back of my house in no time at all—I felt like Bob Vila, and it was good.

No one had ever told me that demolition was much easier than building. No one had explained to me what a weight-bearing wall was. I also had not thought to do more than eye the width of the doors, so I had taken out a few more feet than was needed. As night fell, I had a huge hole in the back of my house and a set of Belgian doors that I had no idea how to install. Then it started to rain—sideways.

Maybe we will finish that story later, but I can report that Connie and I were able to still sell the house a couple of years later. So many times since this event I have tried to be a handyman around the house. I have tried to build fences, install ceiling fans, tear up linoleum floors—you name it. There is this innate desire within human beings that longs to be great at something. This is a God-given desire that pushes all of us toward goals and achievements in our life. I've learned that I should stay away from home improvement, but I believe that my efforts in that area are simply part of the desire God has placed in each of our hearts to become a great artist. By "artist" I don't just mean a person working with brushes and paint, or even with hammers and wood. An artist is someone—anyone—who creates and cultivates. It is someone who can step away and look at her work and know that she created the thing of beauty standing before her. I can see this knowledge in the bright eyes of my two-year-old daughter when she scribbles with crayons but in her mind's eye she is drawing a little girl holding a balloon (I know because she told me so). I can see it in myself—in the eyes a husband who desperately wants to show his wife how much he loves her, but in doing so destroys their home.

We all long to be great at something because the God who created us is an artist, and we are created in his image. The problem is many of us are trying to get great at the wrong things—and some of us are trying to get great at everything. We battle to become great at so many things that it seems like we focus on things in which we are not proficient to the exclusion of that one thing that is really our gift. We will have the opportunity to be good at many things in our lives, and most of the time "good enough" really is good enough. But in a few areas of our lives, God really does equip and call us to be great. We find at least one man who was different.

This man—the hero of this little book—is introduced in 1 Kings 7:13-14:

> King Solomon sent to Tyre and had Huram brought to him. Huram's mother was a widow from the tribe of Naphtali. His father was from Tyre and had been skilled in making things from bronze. Huram was also very skilled and experienced in bronze work. So he came to King Solomon and did all the bronze work. (1 Kings 7:13-14 NCV)

When I read the Old Testament I find that much of what we think is in the Bible, as far as detailed accounts of the personalities and characters of biblical men and women, is mostly conjecture on our part. The Bible does not give us a lot of insight into the thoughts of the patriarchs. So, when I read these stories I like to imagine what *might* have happened—nothing to change theology, mind you, just good imagination at work. It helps the Old Testament characters come alive to me.

As I read this account of Huram I imagine that from a very early age he started hanging around his father's shop and saw what the life of a metalworker was like. He saw the way that people treated metalworkers and how hard his father worked. In the agrarian caste society that serves as the backdrop of 1 Kings, it would be irresponsible for me to suggest that Huram had the opportunities that we have in the twenty-first century. But even in the caste society that Huram lived in one couldn't take away the imagination of a young boy. As his father was working hard I imagine that many times Huram was imagining what life would be like if he were drafted first round in the National Football League (work with me here, it's my imagination). I mean, a son of a tough union metalworker was probably a pretty tough kid himself. I bet he had the build of a linebacker and the mentality of a fullback. I imagine that as Huram began to grow and the child became a young man, reality began to set in. Like every young boy who finally realizes that the red cape will not really make him fly, he was confronted with who he was and the options that he really had in life. In today's world a young man born into poverty can be anything that he puts his mind to being. My dad is a metalworker. After about three weeks of working with him as a teenager it became obvious to both of us that metalwork was probably not a wise career choice for me. Huram probably did not have that choice.

When I was a kid, I really wanted to be a National Basketball Association player. The fact that I stopped growing at five feet ten inches in the tenth grade was not even the reason that I gave up on these aspirations. It was actually the fact that I got cut from the junior varsity team in eighth grade that served as the brutal wake-up call that professional basketball was not in my future. We have all had these moments, these reality checks, when we have to look at ourselves and know that God created us the way we are for a purpose. Unfortunately, it might not be the purpose we wanted it to be. I bet that Huram had that same wake-up call. He didn't have the choice to deny the family business and become a linebacker, but he did have the choice of how good a metalworker he would be. He had the choice to be an average metalworker who would then dutifully pass on the family business to his son, or to be a true artist. It was in this moment that the choice was made and Huram lived before us the artist's mandate.

By the time we meet Huram in 1 Kings 7:13, he is an adult, being called by the king to come and work on one of the largest building projects in the history of the world. He had chosen to get great at something many years ago and finally his opportunity had come.

what is great?

There is a lot of talk these days about being great. There are business books that teach us how to get from good to great; there are "how to" books to help us get great at just about anything in the world. Just the other day I went to a "how to" website and learned how to be great at folding a fitted sheet. The word *great*, like many words in the English language, is distorted by the fact that its scale of use is so varied that it begins to lose its luster.

"How was that waffle?" "Great."
"How was your time with God?" "Great."
"How are you at 'Guitar Hero'?" "Great."
"How are you at surgery, Doctor?" "Great."

Same great word, many great and different meanings. So how in the world are we supposed to define what great is? If we are to be in this wild pursuit of greatness, how do we know when great is great with a little *g* or great with a big *G*?

If the purpose of this book is just to say that we have the potential to be great at something—be it folding fitted sheets or performing brain surgery—then it would be best for me to stop writing and you to stop reading right now. I want to explore how we are to become great not just by the world's standards, but in the eyes of God. If we are to seek greatness for the purpose of becoming a masterpiece in the gallery of worship that shines back to our Creator, then we must start living the artist's mandate. In order for us to truly learn of the "big-G" great, we must follow Jesus and the new concept of greatness that he introduced to the world.

Jesus was teaching his friends about being "big-G" great when he sat them down and told them: "Whoever wants to become great among you must be your servant, and whoever wants to be first must be your slave—just as the Son of Man did not come to be served, but to serve, and to give his life as a ransom for many" (Matthew 20:26-28 NIV).

This whole concept blew the doors off of the daydreams that the disciples had. They had been looking at the cosmic organization chart and saw Jesus at the top, and right below him they had penciled in themselves. It was just a matter of working out who would get the coveted corner office, what the titles would be, and what the 401k would look like. But then Jesus turned the table on all of the daydreams and gave them a picture of what a life of true greatness would look like. Have you ever found yourself wishing that you could do something truly meaningful with your life? That you could be great at something that would leave a legacy? Do you ever find yourself thinking about being great by being a servant to your husband? By meeting the needs of your wife? By washing the feet of your children? By loving your enemies at work and serving your competition on the sales team? This is the new great.

During a small-group session in our home we were taking prayer requests. One couple's request really jumped out at me. Their concern was that where they currently were in life was not where they imagined that they would be. Financial turmoil, some bad decisions, and some tragedy in their lives had severely derailed their plan. This couple has truly been through some of the most trying times that you can imagine. As we sat and talked about what the last year had looked like in their lives, the wife confessed through tears and even some laughter how her preschooler had told her earlier that day, "Mom, I am smarter than you," and how that had just been the straw that broke her emotional back. Listening, I realized that what she really wanted to know was that she was great at something. Currently unemployed and still reeling from the tragedy of losing an infant, she just wanted to know that her life counted. She just wanted to create something of worth, to be great at something. She was forgetting that for the last year she had been a great mom to her two surviving children and a helpmate in the purest sense to her husband. She had not done anything that the world would have considered great. In fact, leaving her high-powered position in the corporate world because of the tragedy in her life was actually not great at all in the world's eyes. But here is the good news: we do not live by the world's standard. We live by Jesus' standard—a new kind of great.

In times like these in my own life I often find myself daydreaming about being a major-league sports coach or player, a rock star, or politician. Maybe I could speak to an arena filled with thousands of people, or perhaps I could write the next best-selling book. (Hey, maybe you're reading it now!) These daydreams always seem to take me on a journey into places that I have never been, and in my dreams I am blessed with skills that I have never had.

I rarely find myself daydreaming about being a great servant—floating away in the clouds about being a better husband to my wife by carrying my weight around the house. It's not often that I daydream about being a great playmate at a park on a Sunday afternoon with my little girl crawling in the dirt, rather than about being a great coach, watching grown men crawling around on the dirt of a football field.

But in order to get great at something, it seems that God intends for us to build upon the foundation of skills and wisdom that he has given us, and not just daydream of skills and talents that we wish we had. He intends for us to use the greatness that he has given us to serve others. What the young mom in my small group needed to hear was that in being a great mom, and a great wife, and the best employee that she can be, she is an artist, creating something of worth within her own family and making an impact on the world around her.

Huram chose to build a masterpiece on that foundation in his life. He was an artist, not because he worked with bronze, but because he chose to get great at something. He used his life to practice and hone his skills and shift from daydreaming to dream-living. It is this shift that makes us artists—when we build on a God-given foundation we become works of art to our maker and others.

As in my earlier story of home improvement, many times we are good at the demolition process in our lives. I have told that story to thousands of people, and what people always remember is that I almost tore my house down. No one ever remembers that eventually we did get the floors down and the Luxembourgian doors installed. We are good at tearing down areas of our lives through rules, regulations, and religion, to the point that we become known for what we are tearing down rather than what we are building.

There are shelves of books that tell you how to get good at things from a demolition perspective. Since the 1980s, the self-improvement aisle at your local bookstore has been growing like a major-league baseball player's arms on steroids. Yet it seems as though this promise of improving oneself has left many empty and void and in need of *more* self-improvement. In fact, it seems that the self-improvement books that promise a "secret" or "eight steps to" simply convince people to chase after yet another dream of being someone that they are not. In many ways these books and methods simply echo the words of the poet laureate of my generation, Dave Matthews, when he asks, "Could I have been a parking lot attendant? / Well, could I have been anyone other than me?"

God desires that we be known not for what we are demolishing, but for what we are building. As Creator, God desires that we too create, that we focus on the things that really matter, lay our foundation on Jesus the rock, and build up those around us as art on display for the world to see.

narrow the focus of your life

Huram was able to narrow the focus of his life. He concentrated. He lived in the sweet spot of the skills, abilities, and opportunities that God had given him. What does this look like? It looks like an administrative assistant who knows that her strength is supporting her leadership and making them look like a million bucks rather than finding ways to improve her own image. It looks like a high-school football coach who knows that encouraging young boys to become young men is far more important than just winning. It looks like a mother who, despite a plethora of professional opportunities, knows that the eighteen years of painting on this blank canvas called her daughter is time well spent.

I was recently having a conversation with my wife and commented to her that I really marveled at the way she has been able to interact with our two-year-old. She is deliberate and focused in her time with her, and it results in such a wonderful, unhurried relationship between the two of them. It also makes my home a marvelous place to come home to. I asked her how it was that she was able to get everything done. Her answer was a great example of an artist at work: "I don't," she said, "I just get the important stuff done." The things that my wife spends time on are what we have determined to be the essential DNA of the Wood home. These things may look very different than your home, but the key is to determine what they are and to focus on them. Here is what this narrowed focus looks like practically for our family, in my wife's role as a mom.

Connie and I were married for ten years before we had our first child. To say that being a mom is the only thing she was created to be would be robbing her of the many roles that she has had, including one I value very highly—her role as my wife, even before we had children. Connie has been and is a great wife. There are many other roles in her life as well that I know she would agree she is good at, but not the greatest. She is a good dental hygienist, a good daughter, and a good small-group leader. After having our first child, however, I have seen that Connie has found a role at which she is truly seeking to be great. Good enough is truly not good enough when it comes to being a mom. I know that Connie spends focused quality time with Isabelle every day. She reads voraciously any article or book about parenting that she can get her hands on. We took four parenting classes at our church in the first two years of Isabelle's life and we talk and pray every day about being the best parents we can be. We see the masterpiece of our children as the greatest offering of worship that we can give to God, and as a beacon of light to the world, our greatest witness and evangelism. Connie's great artistry is made up of many not-so-exciting details. Things such as Isabelle having structured alone time playing in her room while Connie gets household chores done; Connie having a set time to go to the gym every day where she can work out and Isabelle is exposed to other children; learning to use opportunities to teach habits of the heart to Isabelle that will last her a lifetime. These details include nap times, outside playtime, and play dates. They also give the added benefit that Daddy comes home to a very happy and focused family. Like Claude Monet's tiny brushstrokes working together to form a beautiful painting, these details come together into the masterpiece of Connie's parenting. She is a very good mom who is turning into a great mom every day. Why? Because she chooses to narrow the focus of her life. She has chosen to get great at being a mom.

In doing this we have given up a majority of the days that Connie works. This has been a trade-off financially for our family. Connie is not focusing on her career during this season of her life as she was even just five years ago. Choosing to be great at something will mean choosing not to be as good at many other things.

How about your life? Do you feel like my favorite hash browns most of the time—scattered, smothered, and covered?

Are you scattered in your efforts, feeling as though you are so spread out over just enough efforts to be mediocre at all of them?

Are you smothered by a load of papers, demands, tasks, and requests for more of your energy?

Are you covered with guilt about the lack of meaning and influence that you really have in people's lives?

A decision has to be made to be great. You cannot be great at everything, but you have to be great at something. God made you for that purpose.

As any great artist will attest, it is this focus that begins the process of creating a great masterpiece; there are plenty of artists who imagine great works but never do anything.

Getting great at something is simply the first step toward a masterpiece and leads us to the second principle of an artist: **Do something**.

artist's reflection

Every day we have the opportunity to apply this first principle that we see through the life of Huram. We have the opportunity to get great at something and to narrow the focus of our effort in every decision that we make.

: What are a few things that you do well?

: Which of those do you feel has the most influence on others?

: Which of those do you have to manufacture energy to accomplish?

: How can you narrow the focus of your life to the one with the most influence?

: What would it take to be great at that one thing?

artist's reflection

lori fitzgerald

ARTIST PROFILE

A Mom Sculpting a Life before Our Eyes

When Lori and Adam left the doctor's office with their son Michael, their handsome little five-year-old son, the neurologist had just given a baffling diagnosis of world-class proportions. They left in tears and without much hope or useful advice. They left with more questions than answers.

Michael had just been diagnosed with autism.

In the last few years autism has become a household word, with diagnoses soaring, television shows on the topic, and famous actresses writing books on what it's like to be a mother of a child with autism.

No matter how "popular" the disease has become or how much awareness has grown, when it is your little boy that you are hearing about, everything changes in an instant.

It is during moments like this that we have the opportunity to choose between greatness and mediocrity. On that day, Lori chose greatness.

When we think about greatness we often think of athletes, rock stars, and generally people who are quite famous. Lori is not a famous athlete or a rock star. In fact, she is quite shy. I have seen her tell a joke and then blush because she is embarrassed that people are laughing at it. Her definition of a bad day is having attention brought upon her in any way. Every time she reads this book, she will probably blush at the thought of other people reading about her life.

So what is it that she is so great at being? A mom.

When we decide to be great at something, we have to make choices. Hard choices. Choosing to be a great mom is hard work. Choosing to be a great mom to a boy is harder work still. Choosing to be a great mom to a boy with autism is quite honestly very hard. Every choice of words must be scrutinized. Every change of schedule must be evaluated against the effect that it could have on her son's sense of stability and security.

In the same way that an artist who is working on a sculpture must make painstaking and deliberate strokes of his or her chisel to chip away bit by bit at the excess, a mother of a child with autism must make small, deliberate efforts to chip away at the seemingly raw exterior of this little creation to find the beautiful work of art that lies beneath. That is the greatness I have seen my friend Lori express over the last few years. Lori blogs about the adventures of her family—she, Adam, and little Michael, also known as "Frogboy." Take a look at the masterpiece she is creating.

Frogboy Becomes a Cowboy

Tuesday was another amazing day in our house. Frogboy started equine therapy. I have never seen anything like it in my entire life.

It took us about 30 minutes to get there . . . and I got lost 3 times before I actually found the place. We're talking backwoods, people. Anyway, as we're driving in, we notice roosters and hens, cats, dogs, and of course, lots and lots of horses. This is going to be interesting.

See, Froggie doesn't really care for animals that much—although he does like smaller dogs—and he certainly doesn't like being outdoors. He has a hate/hate relationship with dragonflies and butterflies and most other bugs that fly. I figured we had a long day ahead of us.

So we go in and he changes into his jeans, because, as Miss Leslie told him, he's going to be a cowboy today and ride bareback. WHAT?! I really thought the first day would just be, "Hello, this is a horse, see you next week." Anyway, he gets changed and picks a helmet, which takes a few minutes because you want just the right one, and then we're off.

Now I have to say, these people know what they're doing. They should—they do this equine therapy for kids with autism and disabilities alike, so you want to make sure no one gets hurt. But they had Miss Leslie, who was in charge, and then Miss Julie, Miss Susan, and Mr. Rick—one in front, leading the horse, and one on either side, making sure the kid doesn't slide off. Oh, and Danny.

Danny was the horse. Danny was the coolest horse ever. I have never seen such a gentle creature. He was amazing. Again, I'm sure they screen for this, but he was on his mark Tuesday. He sniffed Froggie to get his "stench" (FrogMan's words, not mine), and then they all went to the ring. I got left behind, outside the gate. Story of my life.

Miss Leslie explained some things to Froggie and told him that Danny wanted to play games with him—Danny loves to play games. Froggie found this to be good information. Miss Leslie asked Froggie to mount Danny. Froggie said, "Um, no thanks." Polite kid.

Miss Leslie then explained that Danny really wanted to play, but they couldn't play the games if Froggie wasn't actually ON Danny. They walked through the games without the horse, and my little FrogMan, who can't stand animals or the outdoors or bugs (and there were plenty!) actually RAN over to the horse and mounted up like he's been riding for years! These people really know what they're doing!

Now at this point, I must point out that I was crying and trying to pretend like the wind was causing my eyes to water. I knew if they didn't get FrogBoy on a horse that day, it wouldn't be happening. He's a little like me. But there he was, riding like a pro.

He rode with both hands. Then he started petting Danny while he was riding (he was told to do this, he didn't just start doing it because he felt like it). Then he would reach back and try to touch his tail while riding. He had great posture and would correct himself when he started to slip. He used his voice commands and even learned a non-verbal command for Danny. Froggie was happy. Danny was happy. I was ecstatic.

Eventually they played the games, which were pretty cool. I think Danny was even smiling, although I could have imagined that. Then they had Froggie do a victory lap, during which he actually rode around the ring with both hands in the air—incredible!

All the while, I had Oreo the cat hanging out on top of my feet. And I don't even like cats!

After they were finished, I talked with Miss Leslie and she was very impressed with how well the first lesson went. She actually used the word "miraculous." I think that may be a little strong, but it was nothing short of REALLY COOL.

In the car, FrogBoy told me how proud of him everyone would be. He is so right.

Then he asked me where babies come from. Ruined a great day. I asked him why he wanted to know and apparently he had seen it on a billboard. Thank you, local hospital. Your silly little advertising gimmick has caused me to have acid reflux. Anyway, I asked where he thought they came from, and he said, "From mommies' tummies." Thank goodness I thought to ask before I went into an explanation—his answer was WAY better than mine!

And then, true to Froggie form, he said, "Yeah, they don't come from New Jersey, or lettuce, or mommies' armpits." What a great kid.

Greatness can be defined in so many ways and there are so many opportunities to become great at something. It does seem to me, however, that greatness in Scripture is usually seen as the result of serving someone. Greatness is defined not by how much money we make or by how many people we lead, but instead by the choices we make to change one life. I know that there are thousands of moms who will read this book who feel insignificant—you are great. I know there are thousands of people who will read this book who each and every day serve others in thankless jobs—you are great. My hope is that this book will make it into the hands of someone who feels insignificant and at just the right time they will read these words: "You are great when you serve," and find a new meaning for life.

Every day Lori is striving to be great. On some days, like this one at the horse farm, she really gets it right.

TWO

do something

On a return flight from a pastors' conference, we were about to land back at Raleigh International Airport. I was ready to be home, so the sight of the tops of the North Carolina pine trees made me a happy man. Right about the time that I could have given the flight crew on the ground a high five, the plane's nose went straight up and we went back into the sky at superman speed. Needless to say, this was a little disturbing.

About thirty seconds after everyone on the plane was introduced to what the little white bags in the seat pocket are made for (not just for letting your two-year-old scribble on, contrary to popular belief), the pilot came on and informed us that we were not able to land. Thank you, Captain Obvious.

Apparently fog had set in and the air traffic controllers wanted us to wait a while before landing. This was only the second time that I had flown in my life so the idea that I would have to hang out just floating around in the air was a little disconcerting. About an hour later we noticed that we were starting to do circles around the airport, but unfortunately heard no more talk of descent. It was about that time that the good old boy who had spilled over into my seat for the entire flight decided to give me a little lesson in aviation. He apparently had a nephew in the airline business and reported to me as he continued to squirm around in his seat, "Y'know they only put enough fuel in these things to go an extra hour or so." We would find that his nephew was mistaken. We circled for another hour and a half after that, and there seemed to be plenty of fuel.

It was during those two and a half hours that I learned what the term *holding pattern* really meant. As we rode around and around in the great Carolina sky I felt like the Griswold family spotting Big Ben and Parliament over and over and over again in the movie *National Lampoon's European Vacation*. Although the first few times around it is rather enjoyable and you even like getting to see the same thing twice (it's comfortable, I guess), after a few times you want to break into tears like Clark Griswold and cry, "Help!"

As we journeyed on this airborne cul-de-sac I felt so stuck. I just wanted to do something. It was a very frustrating time.

Life can sometimes seem like a never-ending holding pattern for many of us: the same dead-end job day after day; waking up every morning, grabbing a Krispy Kreme and maybe some Starbucks on the way to work, adding just a few more pounds to the reserve we have already built up. We say in our minds, *We will do something about that one day; eat right, exercise*. Then we do what they pay us to do at work and nothing more, eat some lunch, and then do some more subpar work before we go home to watch bad reality television and SportCenter all night long. After a night of way too little sleep (and we say to ourselves, *We will start going to bed earlier*) we wake up and do it all again the next day. Like a plane caught in an all-too-familiar holding pattern, we are caught in a pattern of doing nothing while staying completely busy.

Surveys tell us that most Americans say that they "hate" their jobs and would do something else if they could. The cliché question often is: "What would you do if you won ten million dollars?" There are so few who would answer that question with a simple, "What I am doing now." In fact, Americans are in an eternal pursuit of freedom to do something, anything other than what they are doing now. In order to gain this freedom we will do just about anything, except "do something" that really matters. We have more stuff than we have ever had, and yet for so many people life is more frustrating and unrewarding than ever before.

As you examine the spiritual, relational, physical, and professional parts of your life, you may feel stuck, like you are in an endless holding pattern, circling the fulfilling life you truly desire. A holding pattern is not God's will for our lives. God does not desire to see his people just circling; God wants us to gain ground and be in deep relationship with him. My prayer is that as you read the first chapter of this book a fire was started in your spirit. I pray that you realized you could get great at something and begin the hard work of creating a masterpiece to glorify God. I pray that you began to get excited about your life for the first time in many years, realizing that your ordinary life could be the extraordinary life you have been looking for all along. The boring white canvas that sits before you can come alive with vibrant colors as God continues to fan the flame of your unique art.

Then, just as you were about to claim your "I M RTST" license plate from the local department of motor vehicles and attach it to your SUV, the nose of your reality jet soared skyward and you were brought back into reality—the reality that you are still stuck in, in many ways. Although you would love to become a better mom, a better dad, a better spouse, or a better worker, you sit back down (figuratively and indeed right back on the sofa) and watch the same game highlight reel for the fourth time in an hour.

it's go time

"Don't put it off; do it now! Don't rest until you do" (Proverbs 6:4 NLT).

Solomon, the king with the sweet crib and temple that Huram was working on, also wrote a couple of books of our Bible. In Proverbs, Solomon offers some wise words on procrastination to a young man caught in a holding pattern—a young man who had been spending a little too much time on the couch. I think the exact term of endearment that Solomon calls him is "you lazy bones." Procrastination is a universal problem. It has existed since the time of Solomon and even before. I have found, in more than a decade of pastoral ministry, that most of us know what we need to do; we just put it off!

We suffer from procrastination paralysis. Maybe you have been there. We call it being stuck, stable, or in a rut. There are a lot of great words for it, but what it really boils down to is that we are not doing what God has called us to do. We are not living out the very life that Jesus saved us to live. Jesus died, was buried, and rose again, defying death so that we can live—not so that we can be paralyzed. I know that I find myself often retreating to the ordinary rather than running full steam ahead like a fullback up against the linebacker who stole his girlfriend. My friend Mark Batterson puts it like this in his book *In a Pit with a Lion on a Snowy Day*: "Your greatest regret at the end of your life will be the lions that you didn't chase." Batterson's assertion is that "normal people run away from lions," but God has not called us to be normal or ordinary. God has called us to be artists and has given us the tools to create a great work of art in his name.

It seems that procrastinating can become a way of life for us. It can become our default. The more we do it, the better we are; some of us are getting great at it. So why do we procrastinate? If we know what to do and why we should do it, why is it that we don't just do something?

We know that we could really be great at something and that if we narrowed the focus of our lives we could accomplish great things for God. We could raise children who would represent Christ to our world; we could be a light to the world in our workplace; we could use our talents to serve our community in ways that would forever change lives. Why then do we let our families devolve until we barely know one another, do just enough at work to not get canned, and look at our community as just the place we live and not as the world we serve?

Why is it that most of us live out our God-given days on earth in this rut of monotony and mediocrity?

some are perfectionists

We set such high standards for ourselves that we never even start. Like a woodworker who is afraid to shave off that very first splinter rather than create a beautiful work of art, we are left holding a block of wood. Solomon describes this attitude using an analogy from the agrarian society to which he wrote: "Farmers who wait for perfect weather never plant. If they watch every cloud, they never harvest" (Ecclesiastes 11:4 NLT).

Solomon paints a picture of a farmer who never plants in his fields because he is waiting for the perfect weather and the perfect way. He goes outside every day and checks the temperature, places a finger in the wind, gazes as the clouds, and chooses not to plant because things just are not perfect. Solomon tells us that if we always wait for the perfect conditions we will never get anything done.

Maybe you are like me and sometimes feel like the farmer in Solomon's story. Several years ago I went through a period of my life where I realized that I was waiting for the perfect conditions to make any move in my life. I was waiting for the next canvas in my life rather than painting the one right before me. I had a dream of being a great man of God, serving God with my entire life, and I had a picture of what that would look like. But when I was in high school I always thought that I would really get serious when I went to college. While in college and single I could not wait to get married, knowing that I would be completed when I got married (thank you, Jerry Maquire). Then as a young married pastor in my first church I thought, *Just wait until I get a little older, then I can really get serious about life.*

This never-ending daydream had started to severely affect not only my future but my current reality. I was putting off getting serious about every area of my life as I waited for the next chapter. All the while, I was leaving blank pages in the early chapters of my life.

Dreams are great, but God works in our reality to create dreams.

As a metalworker, what if Huram had never fired up the foundry but only dreamed of the sculptures in his head? What if Huram's father had not let him mess up many a piece of bronze learning his technique? What if Huram had been so afraid of failure that he had never tried, or had been too lazy to stop watching football and actually act on the skills that his father had taught him and the abilities that God had given him?

Our culture has become much like an episode of *The Simpsons* that I remember watching a couple of months ago. I mean, when I was a teenager. At the end of a typical episode where Homer and Bart had gotten themselves in some kind of ridiculous trouble, Homer sits down with his kids to have a family talk. As he has the children sit down you think they are going to have a moral moment, like when the sappy music would start playing at the end of each episode of *Full House*. Homer looks across at Bart and Lisa and says, "What have we learned here kids? Never try."

Have we gotten to the point where the words of Homer Simpson are truer in our lives than the words of Scripture that tell us, "It's go time"? In order to do this, we will have to fail some. Artists fail. Some failures help create the best works of art. God's glory is the goal—not our perfectionism.

some are afraid

Some of us procrastinate because of fear. This fear of failure gives us an attitude that says, "If failure is an option, we should just not try." "Fearing people is a dangerous trap, but trusting the LORD means safety" (Proverbs 29:25 NLT).

Solomon tells us that the opposite of fear is trust in the Lord. This means that when we are not moving forward and doing something great in our lives for God, the bottom line is we do not trust God. Sometimes it feels like fear can begin to grip us so tightly that we stop breathing spiritually.

My wife and I had been married almost nine years; in fact, it was fifteen days from our ninth anniversary when she told me that she would like to take me out on a date. I love it when my wife takes me out on a date. I am still learning romance and have just recently learned that watching a football game together does not count as quality time, but my wife—she gets it. When she plans a date, I know I am in for a great night. It started with the evidence of how well she knows me when she told me that she was going to take me to one of those "chop it up in front of you" Japanese restaurants, where the cooks are comedians who have that little toy man pee oil onto the flame at some point during every meal. (You have not had fun until a toy pees on your meal!) We got to the restaurant and the night was going great when Connie reached down into her purse and pulled out a small, wrapped package. My heart sank and I began to feel a little queasy as I thought, "Oh no, I blew it. This is apparently supposed to be a celebration of our ninth anniversary." "Babe, I am so sorry," I stammered out, "I did not know this was . . ." But Connie cut me off right there and said, "It's OK, this is for you. It's not an anniversary gift." Feeling a little better, but noting that I should definitely be giving the next "just because" gift, I started to open the small, wrapped package. Guys, have you ever looked at a gift from your wife and been hit with the sudden realization that you have no idea what in the world it is? That was where I was at that moment in the "chop it up in front of you" Japanese restaurant. I panicked. How in the world had everything gone so wrong so quickly? And then it hit me. I had seen enough commercials to realize that the little plus sign on this unknown device made it apparent that this was a pregnancy test—a positive pregnancy test. Barely able to breathe, I looked at my wife and asked, "Is this yours?"

"Yes," she said, "It's definitely mine."

I cannot describe in words the feelings that I felt at that moment. If you are a parent, you understand. I was going to be a daddy. I am wired up to be a dad. I feel like being a dad is the third most important calling I have in my life and something that I am working to be great at every day. Over the next twelve weeks or so Connie and I spent so much time talking about and praying for this new baby. In fact, I was so convinced that she was a little girl that I decided to name her, and every night I would put my hand on my wife's stomach and we would pray for our baby by name. Each and every night we asked God to protect her, to watch over her, and to begin even then to woo her, that she would come to be saved at an early age.

It finally came time in the schedule to go and have our very first ultrasound, and I was so excited. We were on the way to a youth camp, where I was going to be speaking, and planned to stop at our doctor's appointment on the way. We got to the appointment a little early, so the ultrasound technician went ahead and took us back and got Connie set up. Apparently they thought she was a flight risk because they put a seat-belt-looking thing around her; but then they put jelly all over her stomach, which would have made it awfully hard to catch her if she had decided to bolt! Finally they turned on the little television and Connie and I grabbed each other's hands and smiled at each other as we were about to see our little baby girl for the first time.

The screen was motionless.

There was no sound coming out of the speakers.

The look on the face of the technician told us everything.

Baby McKenzie was not alive.

I cannot describe in words the feelings that I felt at that moment. If you are a parent, you understand. I was not going to be a daddy. Connie and I just sat and wept that day as we held each other and tried to make sense of the whole thing.

I am not sure exactly how it happened, but starting on that day I was gripped by fear and lack of trust for God. I had prayed for baby "M" every night. I had committed to becoming a great dad, to pouring my life into the masterpiece unto God that my daughter would become, and it was all gone. I screamed at God as I prayed one night, "God, if you can't be counted on in this, what can I count on you for?" I became paralyzed by fear.

One day, almost three months later, Connie came down the stairs of our home in tears. She was pregnant again and we were scared. I did not even realize it, but over the following nine months I did not pray for my little girl. I was frozen by fear. Then my fear and my distrust of God got even worse—my little girl was born.

I have never seen fear play out in my life so intensely. It was as if everything that I believed about God and had learned through experience with him was thrown out the window when it came to my baby girl. During the first few weeks of her life I came to the place where I realized that fear was holding me back from being the best artist in my family's life that I could be—especially in the life of this new baby who needed a daddy who trusted God. God always finds a way to speak to us, even when we are not actively listening.

A good friend of ours is a painter. She creates "Scripture portraits" in which she uses the pages of old Bibles as the actual canvas and then paints a Scripture verse on it in huge bold letters. Connie and I had been talking with our friend about a four-by-four canvas to go above our fireplace. When our daughter was about a month old we met with our friend at our house to look at samples. As she flipped through her portfolio, she asked a question that God used to expose the sin of fear in Connie and me both: "Is there a special Scripture that you have for Isabelle?"

We did not have a Scripture. Our fear had made us a twenty-first-century version of Adam and Eve, hiding from God the very fact that we had a daughter in hopes that we could keep her safer than God could.

That's when our friend flipped the page at "such a time as this" and we saw it. In big letters on a four-by-four canvas it said: "Trust in the LORD with all your heart." God was speaking through this work of art to teach us that we could be the parents we so wanted to be only if we trusted him. Our fear was a manifestation of our lack of trust.

Every day I come down with Isabelle in my arms to start the day and I see "Trust in the LORD." Every time I feel stressed and feel like I am starting to become paralyzed with fear: "Trust in the LORD." Every time I just need to do something—anything—bold for God I see it: "Trust in the LORD." God has not given us his grace and power to be timid little wimps afraid to do something. We are conquerors.

some are just lazy

"Lazy people want much but get little, but those who work hard will prosper" (Proverbs 13:4 NLT).

Jesus had been the ultimate example of bold action, following his mission uninhibited by fear or sloth. He had worked hard, taught his followers the details of the Kingdom, and now was leading them into the greatest challenge of their time together. Every man needs a circle of friends that he can depend on, and Jesus kept his closest friends near him in the hardest moments. Although up to this time he had requested very little of them other than simply to follow him, that night he would elevate their friendship a notch and request that they help him. "Watch and pray," he told his band of brothers. They all had dreamed of the day when it would be "go time." In fact, just a little later in the story Peter would show that he was ready to "go" when he would cut off the ear of a soldier who tried to take his friend. But that was not the "something" that Jesus had asked him to do. That was not the "something" that Jesus had been training Peter to get great at doing. What Jesus needed was not a soldier but a humble servant. On many occasions he had taught Peter that trust in him and complete dependence upon him was the fight that was worth fighting. It was a fight in his inner soul against the flesh that warred with Peter to "do something"—just anything. But now as his last days on earth drew near he asked the disciples for help. Not to fight, but simply to stay awake and pray. When it really came down to an opportunity to do the thing that Jesus had been training them to do, the disciples were lazy.

I cannot even put on paper the times that I have missed the point just as Peter did, as that list would fill a whole book in itself. I am geared up to be great at something, to do something, to leave a piece of artwork for my master, when I realize that what God is truly asking me to do is so small and seemingly insignificant that I just do nothing.

Jesus had been training them, in part, for this moment of greatness—this moment when they would be there for him and obey him—and in their zeal to do something, they did nothing.

The Roman Catholic Church considers laziness or sloth to be one of the seven deadly sins because it has the power to shut down an entire kingdom. People paralyzed by laziness miss opportunities to be the salt and light of the world. Average people, seemingly insignificant members of the body of Christ, can negatively affect the whole world if they do nothing.

My sister-in-law has diabetes. In layman's terms, diabetes is laziness of the pancreas that affects the entire body. Every single day of my sister-in-law's life has been affected by this seemingly insignificant body part's inability to work for the greater good of the body and just do something.

Far too many of us are causing spiritual diabetes in the life of the Kingdom. It's time to use our gifts and our abilities. It's time to take a chance. It's time to unleash the power of the Holy Spirit in our lives and see what God will do when we simply do something.

stop flying in circles and jump out of the plane

Let's go back to imagining Huram again. I imagine that as Huram focused on taking over the family business and really getting good at something, there were simply days that he felt like he was circling around and around in a holding pattern with an all-too-familiar landscape below him. He was stuck in Tyre. There was already a King Huram in Tyre, so he was stuck being the Huram who was the son of the local metalworker. Day after day and year after year his father kept training him and telling him that this was his duty. Although we do not know if Huram knew the God whose temple he would help build, I know that the God who saves us also puts within each of us a desire to become all that he created and intended us to be. There must have been this God-given desire to be great at something in Huram as well. So year after year he trained. And then one day as a young boy the opportunity came when his father told him the holding pattern of training was over and that it was time to jump out of the plane.

Huram, just like any other young boy, had to be afraid. I remember the first time my Uncle Herbie told me I could drive his truck by myself. For months he had been teaching me how to drive his manual-shift 1984 pickup truck. It was black with a garnet stripe down the side, and he kept it waxed and clean. I was fine with him in the passenger seat, and everything was good, but in the midst of a project we were working on he said, "Shawn, run to the store and pick us up some soda and a few candy bars." (For a dentist, he had a really sweet tooth.) I felt myself get a little sick to my stomach. I could not do this. I was not ready. I would ruin the whole thing. Huram must have felt that way as well. I imagine my Uncle Herbie knew I felt that way. I bet Huram's father knew too.

Our heavenly Father also knows how we feel. God desires to help us push ahead, through the fear, and delights in us when we follow his lead. "When you tell God you'll do something, do it—now" (Ecclesiastes 5:4).

Jesus was very impressed by a group of guys who set aside perfectionism, fear, and laziness to make something happen.

Luke chapter 5 tells us: "One day as Jesus was teaching . . . some men arrived carrying a paraplegic on a stretcher" (vv. 17-18). A little context: Jesus was in a house, teaching. As you can imagine, with Jesus' popularity at this point in his life, the house was packed with people. The Bible does not tell us the paraplegic's name. We just know him as "a paraplegic." But we join this story in progress as the man's buddies were carrying him to the house where Jesus was teaching. These guys were not sitting at home on the couch daydreaming—they were doing something.

They were on a mission. They had heard about Jesus. The paraplegic was their good friend. They grabbed their friend and took him to this house. It was "go time." "They were looking for a way to get into the house and set him before Jesus. When they couldn't find a way in because of the crowd, they went up on the roof" (vv. 18-19). The friends showed up and they knew that Jesus was at the house; the four buddies were literally carrying their friend to Jesus.

What I love about this group of guys is their creativity and get-something-done attitude. They didn't allow imperfect conditions, the fear of failing, or sheer laziness to stop them from getting their friend to Jesus. I have a friend who will do things like this. All of a sudden you hit a dead end and he is the guy like the paraplegic's friend, saying, "Let's take him up on the roof! We will get a running start and jump over the fence, then we can step on the donkey's feeding trough, and the three of us can heave our friend over our heads and get him up there."

I think that most people would have seen this as an opportunity to daydream about what might have been—how it might have happened if they could have just gotten in the door to see Jesus. They may have even gone back to the drawing board and thought of different routes to get to Jesus, but someone had the intestinal fortitude to seize the moment and say, "Let's do something."

The Bible often leaves out details and allows us to use our imagination. How these guys got their friend on the roof is one such case. The Bible simply tells us that next "[they] removed some tiles, and let him down in the middle of everyone" (v. 19). So he was there in the middle of everyone in front of Jesus. And then the text gives a brief but powerful description of Jesus' reaction to the men's behavior: "Impressed by their bold belief, he said, 'Friend, I forgive your sins'" (v. 20).

At that point the religious people got all up in a tizzy. "Jesus, you say you can forgive sins?" they exclaimed, and then they started complaining about what Jesus had done. I hate it when I see myself in the religious leaders of the Bible. I want to see myself like the men who were crazy enough to drop their friend through the roof to get to Jesus, but most of the time I am more like the uptight religious people, scoffing at those whose faith makes them do crazy things.

I pray that as God shapes us and molds us into artists working together on his temple that we will do something—and do it boldly and ridiculously. Jesus did not just ignore the religious people. Jesus rarely ignored anyone. Instead, he answered their protests by making another bold move, telling the paraplegic: " 'Get up. Take your bedroll and go home.' Without a moment's hesitation, he did it—he got up, took his blanket, and left for home, giving glory to God all the way" (vv. 24b-25).

When we do something it leads others to do something as well. This very action continues the mandate: As a follower of Jesus it is my goal to **get great at something,** and then **do something** with my gifts and skills by **investing in things that will last and that will benefit others**.

artist's reflection

In what ways do you feel like you are in a "holding pattern" in your life?

: Is it from procrastination?

: Is it from perfectionism?

: Is it from fear?

: Is it from laziness?

: How can you combat this?

: What would you do if you won ten million dollars and didn't have to work for a living?

: What is something you could do toward this goal starting today?

greg surratt

ARTIST PROFILE

A Normal Guy with a God-sized Dream

The act of simply doing something is easy. Doing something that will have meaning and influence is hard. Doing something that starts a movement is rare. Very few people have the privilege of seeing a movement of God in action. I have the honor and the privilege to be a part of a movement of God. If you have ever been a part of such a movement you know that there are three types of people in a movement:

- There are those who are just tagging along for the ride. They jumped on and are enjoying the scenic route that the movement takes them on, but for the most part they are just bystanders who with hope will one day join in on the real ride.

- Then you have those who are on the ride. Through some set of circumstances and a lot of commitment they have decided to jump in and be a part of something that existed before them, but because of their commitment they have become a real part of the DNA of the movement.

do something

- Then you have the trailblazers. These are the people—usually a very small group of people and ultimately, most of the time one person—who thought, *Why not now?*

Seacoast Church is a movement. I have been able to join the ride and have committed my life to what God is doing here, but if not for one man—Greg Surratt—there would have been no trail to be walked upon. It took one man deciding that people mattered to God enough to give it everything he had and to commit his entire life to chasing after a dream of seeing those people become fully devoted followers of Christ.

In 1987, when it did not make sense and ten thousand people were not showing up, Greg and Debbie Surratt did something huge. They started a dream. If you were to look at the movement now you would think that this was an easy jump to make, but as Greg tells the story it was not always the movement that it is today. In fact, after a great start as a church with more than three hundred people in attendance, Seacoast Church became what Greg calls the "slowest growing church in the country." Dreams do not always work out as fast as we would like them to work out. When the dream starts to look like a nightmare, that is when we have to have faith that we are in the midst of something that is worth our life.

In order to give your life to something, it has to come from a deep conviction. This is where this dream for Greg came from. When he and Debbie could not sit back any longer and watch people outside of a relationship with Christ, they would jump out of the holding pattern and start a revolution and help usher in a movement of God.

Greg was born into a preacher's home. His father was a preacher, his uncle was a preacher, and to be very honest, Greg never wanted to be a preacher. In fact, Greg tells his struggle like this:

My dad brought it; he stomps and hollers and shakes and yells. . . . [He was] brought up in a time with no PA system and did not realize we have those now. My dad sweats when he preaches; in fact, he sweats a lot, and I don't sweat. I really struggled with this fact as God was putting it on my heart to start a church.

Greg often says that at some times in his life he was not quite sure he even liked church, but God had a big plan for him that would include big things. Over the course of several years of being fired as a youth pastor, working for next to nothing in small rural farming towns, and even leaving the ministry for corporate life for a while, Greg was getting to a point that Bill Hybels calls "a place of Holy Discontent." To paraphrase the great Popeye, "He had had all he could stands and he could not stands it anymore!" He knew that he had to *do something*. He knew that he had to give his life selflessly to this passion for the rest of his life.

As a part of this movement that is seeing God change lives every day, I am honored to be riding on the coattails of this man of God who was willing to do something—anything—except sit still.

Greg and Debbie Surratt changed their lives in February of 1988 with sixty-five people meeting in the clubhouse of an apartment complex as they started Seacoast Church. In April of the same year, the first "public" meetings were held in a rented theater with a vision for reaching out to the unchurched people of the Charleston, South Carolina, area.

The dream was to build a church that would speak the language of the modern culture and encourage nonbelievers to investigate Christianity at their own pace, free from the traditional trappings of religion that tend to turn them away. The dream was to see people's lives changed. Greg says often, "I am addicted to changed lives."

Over the next few years, however, God would start to bless this dream and Greg would get to feed his addiction to changing lives. This son of a preacher man would begin to see the opportunities to do something present themselves over and over again in the journey toward the end of the story that is Seacoast.

In 2000 a vision of gargantuan proportions was put before Greg. The way he explains it is that he felt very strongly that God was calling Seacoast Church, this nondenominational church with one location, to start two thousand churches in the next ten years. It was what Jim Collins would call a "Big Hairy Audacious Goal." It was what everyone else would call crazy. Greg often recounts that as he shared this number, he did not know why it had come out of his mouth in front of a large crowd gathered at a first Wednesday service. However, this simple act of doing something brought more people to the team who believed that this dream could be accomplished. In 2001, Seacoast Church, along with several other churches that got behind this dream, started the Association of Related Churches, which will be the catalyst to see thousands of churches started over the next few decades, and most importantly, thousands of changed lives.

In 2001, another God-sized opportunity would present itself to do something huge. God was blessing Seacoast and no one looking in from the outside would have realized this church verging on five thousand people was in a holding pattern. Greg was at a Popeye moment again. As a leader, Greg knew that there were more people in the community than the box could hold and again that was something he could not "stands anymore." The town had recently told Seacoast that they could not build a bigger building, and the truth was no one really knew what to do. The only thing Greg knew was that he had to do something. It was with this addiction to changing lives and a desire to jump out of a holding pattern that Seacoast blazed a trail of being one church in many locations. In order to fit more people into church, Greg led the Seacoast team to do church differently—in multiple locations. Fast-forward seven years, and now Seacoast has thirteen campuses with the capacity for more and more changed lives.

Greg has helped God change lives because Greg chose to do something. We should never underestimate God's power to use our simple act of taking one step forward.

THREE
invest in things that last

Like it or not, you will not live forever—not on earth anyway. This is an alarming revelation for some people. Though statistics clearly show that one hundred out of one hundred dentists agree that we all die, it's hard for us to really believe this fact of death. We try everything we can to extend our lives. In fact, it would seem that Americans, more than any other people in history, are on a never-ending journey to find the fountain of youth. High-school students are being given plastic surgery for graduation gifts and sixty-year-old men and women are stretching, injecting, and flat out destroying their faces in some effort to look forty while forty-year-olds are getting a head start at looking twenty again. We seem to be doing all of this so that we can live longer. But the question that I would have is: Are we doing anything of value with this extra time that Botox and liposuction are supposedly buying us?

The good news is that while our efforts to postpone aging cannot postpone death, we do have a choice about what kind of legacy we will leave behind when we're gone. The bad news is that the picture accompanying our legacy-filled obituary might not be recognizable if we don't quit stretching our faces back and pinning our cheeks to the back of our heads. That aside, we can take comfort that we have the ability to really make a difference in people's lives by investing in things that last—mainly other people.

The entire purpose of this book is that it will help us take steps toward being more like Jesus. As we examine the life of Jesus, we see a man who, though he was 100 percent God, invested fully in the lives of other people even to the point of crawling onto a cross and willingly dying for us. This was the ultimate investment that anyone could make—and he didn't do it for nothing. We need to follow the trail and see exactly what God was investing his son's life into. As we peer through the biblical lens and look at God's portfolio, we find that it is filled with *people*. People just like you and me. Simply put, God's gallery is filled with broken-down people with great upswing potential. We are a group of people who now have the opportunity to grow and expand the investment God made in us by following the model of Christ and investing in others and things that will last.

There comes a point in your life where you have to decide if you will continue to live a life centered on yourself or if you will make the difficult choice of investing in things that will last. Do not be deceived by the ease with which I was able to write and you were able to read that last statement—this is the hardest thing that any human has to do in his or her life. It's a pretty scary moment actually—maybe some of you can remember the moment in your life when you had to make that pivotal choice. You found yourself making a decision based on what was best for another person rather than what was best for yourself. You decided to give away your time, talents, and financial resources rather than look for a way to keep them for yourself. You may even have given up your right to a dream so that the dreams of others close to you could be met. It is during these times of decision that we have to really look inside ourselves to see who we are. We call this process "self-examination" in the area of spiritual disciplines. It's a time when we see who we are and choose to be better or to be worse. There is no staying the same.

In his book *Surprised by Joy*, C. S. Lewis tells how he became a Christian—not coincidentally primarily through reading books. The first step came in 1929 when he was thirty-one years old. He dared to look inside himself and was appalled by what he saw: "a zoo of lusts, a bedlam of ambitions, a nursery of fears, a harem of fondled hatreds." I have looked inside myself many times in moments of decision and seen that very picture: lusts that would have me choose my pleasure, ambitions that would have me treat others like a vehicle to my goal, fears that trap me and confine me to a selfish view of the world, and hate that causes me to hurt others rather than give them hope. It is in my more mature moments that I am able to put these things to death with the help of the Holy Spirit. I wish it were always that I won this battle. My goal is that it become more often.

Many of you have been there or perhaps are even there as you read this book. There is an opportunity before you, and the next step on your journey will be affected by your reaction to this opportunity. It could be a relationship on the brink of death that you are able to resuscitate with the breath of God speaking into your life. It could be comfort and financial stability that you will risk in order to serve others in a faraway land. It is a moment of truth—what will you do with it?

I think that at some point Huram must have looked inside of himself, seen who he was capable of being—both good and bad—and decided that he wanted to live a life that meant something. Putting aside his pleasures, ambitions, fears, and hates, he would choose to have influence that would last far longer than his earthly lifetime. He would make the hard choice to invest in things that would last and that others would benefit from.

one decision

It was probably a pretty ordinary day in Huram's life when he had to make this choice. He got up with the sun, had a cup of coffee and a scone, read the *Tyre Gazette*, and then kissed his mother on the cheek to go and start a day of hard work. In that ordinary life, Huram was exemplifying the first two actions of the artist's mandate. He had gotten good at something and he was doing something with that talent. It was on this ordinary day that Huram got the best news of his career. I mean, let's think about it: he had worked hard, sweated long hours, and had calluses on his hands and sore muscles to prove it. He had done the best he could with what God had given him and where God had chosen to plant him in history. He had worked very hard for a very long time and someone had finally noticed.

That someone was King Huram of Tyre, the one after whom our Huram had been named. King Huram had been contacted by King Solomon of Israel to provide him with some of the awesome building materials Lebanon had to offer, as well as some talented artisans skilled in working with those materials. King Huram replied, praising the God of Israel and commending our Huram by name, saying he was skilled enough to complete any project assigned him, from bronze and ironwork to goldsmithing and engraving to working with delicate and expensive fabrics. With this recommendation to end all recommendations, Huram was being presented with the chance to work on one of the largest building projects in history.

As we read it today, Huram's choice seems like a no-brainer; but let's imagine a little again. I imagine that Huram was just starting out on some of the first work of the day when a messenger arrived at his shop. He came to let him know that the king had chosen to send him to Israel to work on one of the biggest and highest-profile building projects of the millennium. There were a lot of things to do at Huram and Sons that day. There was a stack of bills to pay, a lot of invoices that needed to be processed, and a ton of metalwork to be done. Just that morning, Mr. Obenidite (well, what do you think—his last name would have been Smith?) had called again asking about his new porch railings that Huram had been meaning to get to for weeks now. The Obenidite family paid well. Now he had two kings wanting him to go be a part of the church construction Dream Team. Would it pay as well? Sometimes churches even want you to volunteer. How would he get all of the work at Huram and Sons done? Who would take care of his mom and all of his day-to-day duties in Tyre? Then there was the whole Tyre Tigers football season that he would miss (OK, I am getting carried away in my imagination, but I bet there were at least lion fights or something). If Huram was anything like me, he thought through this proposition, and some selfish thoughts had to have crept up: *Someone else can do it. Surely in all the land of Israel there is a bronzeworker who can do the job. . . . How much will Solomon pay me for this gig? . . . Will my name be famous? Will people finally stop confusing me with the King? . . . Traveling all the way to Solomon's would be a real pain in the butt!*

I know I am not supposed to say this, being a pastor and a Christian author, but let's be real for a couple of sentences here. It does seem like a lot of the time, when God presents us with life-changing opportunities to invest in things that matter, they look like a pain in the butt—more specifically, a pain in *our* butts. They are usually not the most practical or self-serving options available. I lean toward self-serving. I lean toward what would be the best thing for my family and my goals. I lean toward a painless butt.

a story of selflessness

I want you to imagine with me being forty-four years old. You have four children and a wonderful wife. You work hard to make a living, and pour everything else that you have into your family. You are a leader at your church; you are on town council; and you are seen as the head of a model family.

One of your daughters is sixteen. Like most sixteen-year-old girls, she is dating a guy you could do without. You think he is a punk who is trying to steal her heart. In fact, you are pretty sure he already has. You have tried to discourage her, only to have her rebel, and now that little girl who you used to get smiles and hugs from is running to another man. You don't like it, but what can you do? She is breaking your heart, but you work from 7:00 a.m. to 8:00 p.m. five days a week and it's the best you can do just to keep up with your six-year-old son and the yard work. This guy will eventually go away, you reason. "Raise up a child in the way," right? Surely she'll ditch him soon. But she does not ditch him, and he does not go away.

Late in the summer of your daughter's sixteenth year, she comes to you in tears and tells you a story you don't want to hear. The guy and she had gone too far. It was the summer and there had been too much free time, and now there is a problem—your baby girl is going to have a baby herself.

Some of you don't have to work very hard to imagine the story. In fact, many of us have lived this story in some small way.

When I was in grade school I used to read stories that were called *Choose Your Own Adventure* novels. You may have read these too. Those were great books. You would get to a place in the book that was a moment of decision, where a choice had to be made. You would have several of these decision-time opportunities throughout the book. What I really enjoyed about these books was that in the end it would be my choices that would decide the fate of everyone involved. I loved these books. I liked being able to choose and see the results play out. Yes, I have always been a little bit of a control freak.

This story is the first chapter to the "choose your own adventure" story that is my life. The forty-four-year-old father of four was my grandfather, and the sixteen-year-old girl was my mother. In this adventure, the choices my grandparents would make that day, when their sixteen-year-old daughter came into the room in tears, would be choices that would decide my fate and the fate of my mother. A choice had to be made.

Remember, there comes a point in your life where you have to decide if you will continue to live a life centered on yourself or if you will make the difficult choice of investing in things that will last. It seems that often the choice is made to continue a self-centered life, to selfishly invest in our own fleeting whims instead of something of lasting value. In many ways, this selfishness can destroy our lives.

In the book of James, particularly the fourth chapter, the Bible gives us a glimpse into ourselves and into the battle that often rages deep down inside of each of us. To be honest, James takes out a wooden spoon and pops us on the hand.

Where do you think all these appalling wars and quarrels come from? Do you think they just happen? Think again. They come about because you want your own way, and fight for it deep inside yourselves. You lust for what you don't have and are willing to kill to get it. You want what isn't yours and will risk violence to get your hands on it.

You wouldn't think of just asking God for it, would you? And why not? Because you know you'd be asking for what you have no right to. You're spoiled children, each wanting your own way.

You're cheating on God. If all you want is your own way, flirting with the world every chance you get, you end up enemies of God and his way. And do you suppose God doesn't care? The proverb has it that "he's a fiercely jealous lover." And what he gives in love is far better than anything else you'll find. It's common knowledge that "God goes against the willful proud; God gives grace to the willing humble."

So let God work his will in you. Yell a loud *no* to the Devil and watch him scamper. Say a quiet *yes* to God and he'll be there in no time. Quit dabbling in sin. Purify your inner life. Quit playing the field. Hit bottom, and cry your eyes out. The fun and games are over. Get serious, really serious. Get down on your knees before the Master; it's the only way you'll get on your feet. (James 4:1-10)

The message of Jesus is undoubtedly good news, but as James lays out, there is a challenge that comes with this good news that is quite necessary, yet extremely hard to swallow.

A friend of mine once sent me a link to an article about Buckley's Cough Mixture, which has been very popular in Canada since 1919. I did a little research on it and found out that, unlike many companies that load their products down with corn syrup, sugar, and artificial flavoring to make their medicine palatable, the manufacturer of this cough syrup does absolutely no such thing. In fact, the long-standing battle cry of the company has been that Buckley's may taste bad, but it works. Consider one of their advertising blurbs (slightly adapted): "If you are inquiring about your cough mixture tasting like expired milk, trash-bag leakage, a postpedicure foot bath, a state fair portable tollet, decomposing meat fat, monkey sweat, used denture soak, New Jersey, or hippie-festival runoff, please hang up. Your cough will be gone shortly."

In those moments when I am tempted to choose to be myself, I remember the experience I had when I first read James 4:1-10, and I realize that sometimes I don't like the way the Bible tastes, but the cure it provides is well worth the temporary grimace.

I wish that I could read the Bible and always feel like I have it together, but the truth is many times when I read the Bible I realize the truth about myself and I realize that I am the problem. I am often confronted with the opportunity to make that choice to decide if I will continue to live a life centered on myself or if I will make the difficult choice of investing in things that will last.

I learned a lot about this dilemma when my little girl was two years old. Many of you have had a two-year-old in your home, and I think that you will agree with this assessment: We all have a two-year-old within us who is waging a war!

I think we can safely say that most two-year-old children are pretty much hardwired for selfishness. I never once remember teaching my little girl to say, "No, Mommy" or, "Go away, Daddy." It just came naturally. I especially remember when a whole new set of words showed up in our home as Isabelle really started acting like a two-year-old.

There was a period of time when my little girl loved to buckle and unbuckle things. Any time she would climb out of her "eat seat" (that's our family name for the high chair) she would start saying, "bucklebucklebuckle" at a frantic pace. There was much drama involved. I think she got the drama from her mama.

I remember one time while playing in the backyard she ran over to her swing; I started to reach down to unbuckle the seat to let her in when she declared, "No, Daddy; Ihhh-bell do-eat." ("No, Daddy; Isabelle do it.") I quickly learned that Isabelle was acting her age, and that part of my job was to help her grow up.

I can't help realizing that although I am thirty-one years older than my little girl, I still often act like a two-year-old. Sometimes I feel like there is still a two-year-old who battles within me. When I am working on a team at work, sometimes I just want to scream, "Shawn do it!" When I am at home and my wife has the remote control, sometimes I want to snatch it and run as fast as I can, screaming, "Mine, mine, mine." There is a two-year-old within me screaming and crying every time I do not get my way, a two-year-old within me who stomps and pounds my fists at God for all that I don't have, and a two-year-old within me who at every opportunity seems to run away at top speed from the Father who loves me who is trying to protect me from the arms of sin. When I let this two-year-old have his way, it is called selfishness. James tells us two things about this two-year-old.

1. We want our own way and we want it now.

"Where do you think all these appalling wars and quarrels come from? Do you think they just happen? Think again. They come about because you want your own way, and fight for it deep inside yourselves. . . . You're spoiled children, each wanting your own way" (James 4:1, 3b).

I love James's straightforwardness here. You want to know why all of the stuff that is happening in our world is happening? It's because of me! Before you let yourself off the hook too soon, it's because of you, too. Like a two-year-old who wants her way, we too make decisions that are based only on what is best for ourselves.

What if my grandfather had chosen what was best for him and sent my mom away? What if my mom had chosen to use the newly legalized abortion option and never go through the grief of telling anyone? What if my aunts and uncles had dismissed me as a mistake to be ashamed of rather than a blessing to be thankful for? Their choice to be radically selfless changed my life, and quite frankly, the lives of thousands of people to whom I have had the opportunity to minister. In fact, the choices of these people have changed your life in at least one small way—you are reading a book by someone who was seen as a worthy investment rather than a mistake.

Huram could have chosen what was best for him. He could have demanded a better assignment on the project, working on a piece of the project that would be seen by more people, rather than the very tops of the temple columns. He could have decided to stay in Tyre and build his business. He could have never even gotten great at anything to begin with, and just lived for the moment. But instead, he made a choice that we study and write books about thousands of years later.

2. We want what is not ours.

"You lust for what you don't have and are willing to kill to get it. You want what isn't yours and will risk violence to get your hands on it. You wouldn't think of just asking God for it, would you? And why not? Because you know you'd be asking for what you have no right to" (James 4:2, 3a).

Greed is really one of the basic sins that we all struggle with. From the time we are born until the time we die, we are daily confronted with wanting what is not ours. One of the things that we lust for the most is fame. Fame belongs to God. God alone deserves it, yet we all are willing to kill for fame. Now if you are like me, you immediately think that is an overstatement. *Surely you jest*, you're thinking. *I would not kill for fame.* The first time I really read James 4 and pondered this very idea I thought the same thing. Then I heard these questions in my heart of hearts.

Would you not kill coworkers' dreams for your fame?
Would you not kill relationships for your fame?
Would you not kill yourself spiritually for your fame?

With the answers to these questions, I look inside and see, like Lewis, a "zoo of lusts" that aim to take what I do not deserve, rather than a gentle spirit that looks to invest in things that truly matter. With this knowledge I feel lost, but God gives us more grace: "That is why Scripture says: 'God opposes the proud but gives grace to the humble.' Submit yourselves, then, to God. Resist the devil, and he will flee from you. Come near to God and he will come near to you" (James 4:6-8a NIV).

I know that Huram must have struggled with this as he made the decision to work on Solomon's high-profile building project. He would have the chance to get his name in lights, or at least in bronze. I know that he must have felt this inner struggle to do what was best for him and his future legacy. We will see in the next chapter that Huram stepped up to the plate and chose to invest in things that might not bring fame and fortune, but that would last, and he chose to even work on some things that would never be seen by anyone but God.

and now the rest of the story

My forty-four-year-old grandfather and grandmother had some choices to make. The odds were stacked against me in the first chapter of my life story, and their choices could lead to destruction or to a legacy.

The first choice that my family had to make was to choose life. It was the summer of 1973. That date may not mean a whole lot to you, but as a child born to a seventeen-year-old girl from a "perfect family" living on "Perfect Family Lane" in the spring of 1974, it has always had a little extra meaning for me.

In January of 1973, just five months before I was conceived, the Supreme Court ruled that it was legal to abort an unwanted baby. I would say that at that point in time, I would have fit into the "unwanted" category.

I have never really asked my family for the details of this choice, but the best evidence of their decision is right here—they chose life.

Since I was a teenager I have had people ask me after hearing my story, "How did you get fixed? I mean, everything was against you, right? How did you turn out to be a pastor?"

Here is my answer and it is the absolute truth: I never knew I was broken.

My family decided to invest in a human life, rather than in fleeting things like reputation or comfort. They made some very selfless decisions.

I had a grandfather, Papa, and a grandmother, Nanny, who took me in as their own. They decided that I was going to be something. They decided that they would leave a legacy through the life of a child.

There was a young college-aged couple—Aunt Karen and Uncle Herbie—who treated me like I was their child even though they were in the middle of college life. When others were at fraternity parties, pouring beer and shots, they were pouring energy and love into my life.

I had an uncle, Lamar, who was only seven when I was born. He became my big brother.

At the age of nine, I met the man who would become a dad to me, Cliff. I saw him take care of a family and work hard. I saw him pay for my college education when he could have said, "He's not mine." But instead, he introduces me as his oldest child and often jokes about how much we look alike.

I had a mom who chose to be a mom at seventeen years old; a mom who invested her life into making sure that I was taken care of; a mom who to this day lives ten houses down and is helping now to raise my child. She gave up a lot. And yes, I know that many would say that it was a consequence of sin, but I have never really liked being referred to as a consequence. I like to see myself more as a blessing that came out of a sin-filled situation. My mom saw that too.

Because of my family's investment in me, I grew up believing that I was as normal as normal could be. I never even heard the term "broken family" until I was an adult. Nowadays we take our kids to classes to learn how to function in a broken family; we give them a list of reasons, backed up by research, of why they can't possibly be OK; and we are ready to call them "broken" before they are even born. It doesn't have to be this way.

I was getting my hair cut one time and struck up a conversation with a single mom who I found out attended my church, Seacoast Church. She told me about her son, and how she was relatively new to the area after moving here a couple of years before, following her divorce. Then she told me something so cool. She told me about three guys in their twenties and thirties from my church who come and pick her son up a couple times a month, just to hang out with him and invest in the man he will become. They are not a part of a group that is doing this; no one begged them to help out; they are not getting any recognition; but they have chosen the hard choice of living a worthy adventure, leaving a legacy that will survive long after they are gone.

Nichole Nordeman says it best in her song "Legacy":

I want to leave an offering,
A child of mercy and grace who blessed Your name unapologetically.

When we choose to live selflessly and invest in things that last, we can change our world and leave a true legacy. In the final two chapters of this book we will explore the legacy that Huram left and how our choices continue the artist's mandate: As a follower of Jesus, it is my goal to *get great at something*, and then *do something* with my gifts and skills by *investing in things that will last and that will benefit others*. In living this lifestyle I will *work for an audience of one*, because I understand that sometimes only God will see my best work.

artist's reflection

Every day we have the opportunity to apply this third principle that we see through the life of Huram. We encounter opportunities to invest in others and ultimately leave a legacy.

: We will all die one day. Given this fact, who will be different because you lived?

: How does pride and selfishness keep you from truly investing in others?

: What opportunities do you have in front of you to be self-serving?

: What opportunities do you have in front of you to invest in others and leave a legacy in their lives?

: How can you learn to choose service to others over service to yourself?

artist's reflection

herbie orvin

ARTIST PROFILE

Husband, Dad, Coach, Missionary

As I stepped behind the pulpit, it was both one of the most honoring and most mournful times of my thirty-three years of life. The past three days had been an absolute emotional whirlwind. In a time when the natural thing to do was weep, for the past seventy-two hours I had been strong. I had to be strong to make it through one of the most important sermons of my life.

On a Monday morning, my dad called at around 8 a.m., and he told me that he had gotten a rather upsetting phone call from my Aunt Karen, who frantically told him that she was following an ambulance that was taking my Uncle Herbie to a local hospital. He was only fifty-one years old. Less than thirty minutes later, while driving to the hospital, I learned that he was dead. When I arrived at the hospital there were already more than two hundred people from the community there, just because they knew they had to be there for this family. These were just the two hundred people who had learned in the previous hour what had happened. In the coming days these people and many more would tell a story of a man who had invested in their lives.

As I stepped behind the pulpit of the church, it was to preach the funeral of a man who had invested in my life. In many ways a father to me, my Uncle Herbie showed me so much love throughout my life, and I soon found out that he had invested in many other people as well, having a profound influence on countless lives. He was a man who had become great at many things, but most of all it was what he did for others that made him a great man. He was a great husband. He was a great dad. He was a great neighbor and community leader. He was a great dentist. Most of all, he was a great example of Christ.

Over the three days between his death and his funeral, we saw some amazing returns from this investment that my Uncle Herbie had made in people. There was a line nearly a half-mile long as close to ten thousand people tried to come and pay their respects to his family at the funeral home. At the funeral the church building was packed, with many people standing outside just to make sure they were there. Over those three days, we heard stories from people that absolutely blew me away, revealing a life of service, selflessness, and investment in others that surprised even those of us who knew him well.

As I write a book about what it would look to have a life of meaning and influence, Herbie Orvin is one of those iconic figures that I cannot get out of my head.

This picture was painted by a series of stories. This small excerpt from my cousin's application essay to law school truly shows the power of investing in others' lives.

Growing up, I had a life that one might consider almost perfect. I was blessed with a father and mother who loved each other and their children deeply, a close extended family, and two brothers who are more like my best friends. My father, a well-respected local dentist, spent much of his time investing in our community, young people, and athletic programs while my mother, a highly requested elementary teacher, taught at our local school. There was not a Friday night we were not in the stands at our high school football, basketball, or baseball games, and there was never a local young person who needed support that my father did not provide. He believed that athletics was more about the people playing than the games themselves. Believing that everyone should have the same opportunities, my father did his best to provide what he could for those around him who needed support.

The following stories continue to paint a picture of the themes that so encapsulated the life of this man.

Faithfulness. The first story was with my aunt soon after we returned to her home from the hospital. We were sitting in her room, just the two of us, and we were talking a little, but mainly just sitting. She grabbed a blanket from her bedside, saying she was cold, and then she started to weep. Over the next few minutes, she would recount to me the morning routine that her husband had followed for most of their married life. My aunt is always cold. She is cold in the summer lying by a pool. I have honestly seen her throw a blanket over her legs at the beach! Herbie knew this and he would wake up every morning and get up just a few minutes before her and start a small space heater in the bathroom to get the room warm. He would start the shower to make sure the water was hot by the time the "princess," as he called her, got ready to take her morning shower. After he got her set upstairs, if it was cold outside he would go and start his wife's and his daughter's cars so that the cars were ready when needed. He was faithful in every way that a husband could be. He was a best friend, a confidant, and someone my aunt always knew would put her first. Even the night prior to his death they had spent together, because he had chosen to be with her. She needed to go to the store on a late-night "because-we-are-empty-nesters" run, and rather than staying at home and watching ESPN Classic one more time, he tagged along and they talked. He invested in his wife, his family, his church, and his community—and was faithful to these. He invested in things he knew would last, and they are still a trophy of his faithfulness.

Selflessness. At some time during the days following my uncle's death, we opened the garage. The mess would have horrified pack rats. His sons told me that was the way he liked it. He said he knew where everything was and that no one could possibly steal something because they would not be able to find it. What was really strange was the amount of "junk" that was in the garage. My uncle was a dentist. I was pretty sure he was not running a Sanford and Son's type of business out of his garage, so it intrigued me as to what the deal with all of the junk was. As I asked around a little, I finally got an answer from my aunt.

Herbie lived in a rural area and saw it as one of his "callings" in life to help people. In fact, after many a message on "missions" at church he would tell people he was called to be a missionary to Macedonia (the rural town in South Carolina, not the biblical city). Herbie would learn of people in need and would want to help them financially, but he told his wife that to protect people's pride he would offer to buy something from them. For example, he purchased an old broken lawn mower for as much as it was originally worth and a rusty bike he did not need, which did not even work, for fifty dollars. What would have otherwise been seen as junk had now become trophies of selflessness.

Character. People who invest in other people and in things that last have character. It just goes hand in hand. Character is a hard word to define, but it is best seen in action. My Uncle Herbie believed in character. It was the cornerstone of every decision that he made in his life. This belief in the importance of character was something he inherited from his family, and was one of the investments in his eternal portfolio. In fact, one of the first elements of the funeral service was the testimony of three African American men who had grown up in rural South Carolina with the Orvin family. The testimony of these three men was that Herbie's father, Harry Orvin, had been one of the first white men in the small community of Macedonia and Alvin to stand up in favor of the desegregation of the public school. These men told a moving story of Harry bringing his two sons into the "colored" side of dressing room and providing the young men with the same cleats as the white boys had, rather than the intended hand-me-downs. Character was something that this family knew mattered and they invested in the character building of others. Character was not just a word to Herbie Orvin; rather, it was something that was built by a lifetime of choosing to do the right thing, even when the wrong thing was much easier. This character affected every single area of his life. His business was run in such a way that he put the needs of people first and the dollar second. He taught me a lot about character through his words, but most of it I learned by watching him choose to do the right thing for people.

I am not sure that a small chapter in a small book can possibly give justice to this man and to the principles by which he lived. In fact, my fear is that there are no words to truly describe what he did for me, and certainly it would take an entire book to relay all of the stories I heard just in those three days. My hope is that after reading just this small slice of one small man, you will be changed. My hope is that you will take a look at your relational portfolio in a new light and start to look for opportunities to invest in the people God has planted you near. My hope is that you will leave a legacy.

FOUR
work for an audience of one

As I mentioned earlier in this book, I do not have strong carpentry skills. To be honest, that admission is an understatement akin to a hippopotamus stating that he does not have strong aviation skills. As poor as my carpentry skills are, however, it seems that, as a homeowner, I often find myself in situations where I am on a ladder trying to install, paint, or in some other way destroy something. During these moments, it becomes painfully obvious what people really believe about their work.

In our home we have a fifteen-foot vaulted ceiling in the living room area. You can look down from the second story. This will be great for water-balloon dropping when my children are a little older. For reasons that I don't even recall (probably because I blocked them from my memory) I have been on the top rung of a ten-foot ladder and seen the sheetrock of our high ceiling up close. At the risk of being the hippo now criticizing the eagle's flight pattern, I have to say that it's just not good workmanship. It's not straight. There are places where the putty is peeling off, and in several places you can see that there was no sanding of the surface before painting. These were very small blemishes (at least until I tried to fix them) but most assuredly not the best work of professional craftsmen. No one would ever be able to see these flaws from the floor of the house unless they had a telephoto lens (which would be rather strange to have in one's home); so theoretically, the outward appearance of the work is great. The craftsmen got paid for their work and moved on.

On another occasion I installed a new microwave oven in my kitchen. (By "I installed" I mean that I called my dad, who came down with his tools, and I watched from across the room so as to not get in the way.) We were putting the microwave into the same place where the oven ventilation had been. As we took off the vent it looked as if a drive-by nail-gun shooting had occurred. There were three dozen or so nail holes in the plasterboard behind the vent where the workman had used the "shoot then aim" method of finding the studs. *No one will ever see the wall behind the oven vent*, he probably thought. *What does it matter if it's not my best work?*

Huram was in a similar position. As he climbed higher and higher onto the top of the rickety scaffolding and started to look down on all the people polishing the floor tiles and carving the furniture, he must have felt like he was a million miles away. I imagine, because I am a little odd, that he started humming Dave Matthews's "Ants Marching" as he looked down at all the little people of the world.

The Bible tells us exactly how high off the ground the tops of these columns were, and as best I can recall from the one semester of Hebrew I took, the rough translation is "really high." A less rough translation reads "thirty-four feet high." I imagine that most people reading this book would pass out just thinking about climbing thirty-four feet in the air, but that's just a guess from a guy who is afraid of heights. Men wired up like Huram like "really high." My dad is a metalworker like Huram, and the liking for things "really high" must come from breathing the smelting fumes or something because he actually enjoys walking across two-by-fours hung by dental floss thirty or forty feet off the ground. He laughs at all of us who are closing our eyes as we watch from the ground. Huram was that kind of guy.

200 pomegranates

So there was Huram, in a place where only people with a fume-induced disregard for common sense were going to be, and he was faced with yet another choice. As he was looking down on all of the people walking by, it had to be obvious to him that he might very well be the only human to ever see this work. For just a moment imagine the columns leading into the temple courts. Do you see them? OK, now look at the very top of the columns, thirty-four feet in the air. Now imagine that you have to do some work on the top of the columns—twice as high as my sheetrock guys had to work. Every day, hundreds, maybe even thousands of people will walk past these columns. Every day they will look at them as they enter the temple. For centuries these columns will be seen by tens of thousands of people—at right about eye level. You are probably holier than me so this has not crossed your mind, but if I had been Huram I would have put 95 percent of my effort into the carvings that went around the columns at about three cubits high. Let's be honest, I would have put 100 percent of my effort into three cubits high. For those of you who do not do cubits, that is about six feet high. I would have carved all of the intricate designs and elaborate sculptures right where everyone could see them. The ladies would have embroidered their dresses with my designs, and I probably would have gone down to the Christian bookstore and bought one of those little silver do-dads like you sometimes see nailed to the backs of church pews, to announce that this column was "Crafted by Shawn. In Honor of Shawn." Everyone would have known what I could do. This had to cross Huram's mind. But that's not what Huram did.

> First, he cast two pillars in bronze, each twenty-seven feet tall and eighteen feet in circumference. He then cast two capitals in bronze to set on the pillars; each capital was seven and a half feet high and flared at the top in the shape of a lily. Each capital was dressed with an elaborate filigree of seven braided chains and a double row of two hundred pomegranates, setting the pillars off magnificently. He set the pillars up in the entrance porch to The Temple; the pillar to the south he named Security (Jachin) and the pillar to the north Stability (Boaz). The capitals were in the shape of lilies. (1 Kings 7:15-22)

Huram was definitely not thinking like an entrepreneur or a publicist. He didn't seem to care that most people wouldn't even notice the fancy bronzework at the very tops of the columns. Even if they did crane their necks to gaze at the decorative capitals, they wouldn't be able to make out the details that distinguish a lily from a palm branch or a pomegranate from an orange. But he resisted the temptation to put effort only into the things that would earn recognition and praise. In studying this passage, I think it would be a little of a stretch to say that we know as a matter of fact that Huram did all of these things to worship God. However, it is with this unbelievable choice that I am drawn to believe that something happened to Huram while he was working on this project. At some point, all the getting great, doing something, and investing in others had pointed him in the direction of God, and it seems that with this act of selflessness, he was somehow worshiping God. Huram faced the temptation that we all face so often in life, but something bigger than himself seized his heart and he made a choice to do his best work as unto God.

This is the temptation toward pride and self-centeredness that is at the root of all sin. We want to get great at something. We want to do something. We even want to invest in things that will last, contributing something of beauty and value to the world. The rub comes when we do all three of those, and then we want everyone to know about it. We look for this recognition because *we all have a need for acceptance.*

Regardless of our age, our maturity, or even our status in life it seems that we all long for someone to tell us that we did a great job. We long to hear our spouse tell us that we look great and that we indeed do not look fat in those jeans, our children tell us that they are proud of us, our bosses tell us that they appreciate us, and our coworkers acknowledge that we are important to the team's overall success. We all want to receive the reward, we all want the blue ribbon, and we all want a whatever-of-the-year bumper sticker on the back of our car. Some need it more than others, especially those with a strong "words of affirmation" love-language like me, but even the hardest of people need to be told, "People like you; and darn it, you are special!"

This is a God-given need placed in our DNA by a Creator who wants to be the one to give us the hope and encouragement that we all so desperately need. But when we let this need begin to drive us away from God and into pursuits of selfishness, we see that we all have an inward battle with pride.

we all have an inward battle with pride

Not to be a real downer here, but all of you who read that statement and thought, *I am not prideful; I am humble*, well, you have just proved my point. We all lean toward moments in our lives when we become, as the Scripture says, "wise in our own eyes." This false wisdom that the Bible calls "foolish" is pride. Pride is the root of all sin. In fact, we see pride start to show its ugly head early in the Genesis story line, and it continues to show up in our very own hearts. In Scripture, through history, and even in the journey of our own lives if we were to look closely, we would see that those who choose to follow this pride end up with a life void of meaning or influence. They end up with a life that is centered on themselves and their lives, and in the end, they end up utterly alone. Some of the most talented, skillful people in the world—people who have gotten great at things and really done some stuff—miss the purpose of this talent and end up spending a life lacking in real substance. In order to truly fight against pride we must be able to get the long view of our lives. We must be able to look ahead and see what the story looks like even after we are gone. We have to be able to look from God's view.

Have you ever looked through a View-Master? I love those things. I recently used a View-Master as an illustration in a sermon. I went to the store expecting to find the 1978 version of a View-Master that I had as a child, and boy, have things changed. They have Dora the Explorer View-Masters, Batman View-Masters, and even View-Masters in the shapes of tigers and elephants, but after searching all the retail stores in my area I could not find a classic red View-Master anywhere. So I bought a Dora View-Master since I have a little girl. (Every daddy with a little girl will give into the Dora madness eventually.) Although it looked different on the outside, it still worked the same. You put in a wheel and click the button and depending on the wheel that you put in, the view will be different. If you put in a Batman wheel, you see Batman. If you put in a Dora wheel, you see Boots and Diego and, of course, Swiper saying, "Ahhh Man!" In our lives we have a few different wheels from which we can choose. We have one wheel that is from the perspective of the trio of me, myself, and I. We see life from this perspective when we are letting pride lead us. Then there are other times when, in a valid attempt to see from a different perspective, we put in the wheel that gives us the perspective of them, they, and those people. We worry so much about what others think and what "they" need, think, or care about that we begin to build our lives around the wrong perspective. It is only when we can see life from the view of Jesus in Scripture, God through history, and the Holy Spirit in our hearts and minds that we can see the proper view of things. It's when we ask ourselves questions like, *What does Jesus say about this in Scripture?* or *What is the Holy Spirit leading or prompting me to do?* and *How does this represent the character of God through history?* that we are seeing the long view.

Sometimes I think I get stuck on the "me" reel in my life. A selfish view of our lives becomes a one-sided perspective that can leave us empty and void of so many other grand views in life—mainly God's. In order to truly live a life of meaning and influence we have to be able to change the view in our lives and see from God's perspective. We need to change our perspective, see life from thirty-four feet high on the top of some shaky scaffolding, and take the long view—God's view—of our lives. If we can get beyond our pride-filled view of our own selves, we can gain the wider, more godly, peripheral vision needed to see other people, and to do things to serve others that may or may not be noticed by others but will definitely be noticed by God.

we all want to have influence

In our families, at our jobs, and mostly within our thoughts during very quiet moments, we all want to believe that we are needed in order to make the world turn around.

It is a very lonely place to be when you realize that if you didn't show up tomorrow, the world, your home, your workplace, and your community would be exactly the same. It is during those lonely moments that we all realize, despite all of the wealth we may accumulate, despite the power and prestige we may gain at work, and even in spite of how much we may love God, our most basic desire is to have some influence on our world. When we feel that we are not having this influence, our inner two-year-old comes out and we demand any attention we can get. It is often during these times that we feel the need to carve some pomegranates right in people's line of sight, just so they will know we do *something*; just so we will know that we are there!

Think of the mom who feels invisible. I'm sure you know one. Maybe you even are one. She takes out the trash; no one notices. She does the laundry and dishes; no one notices. She cooks meals; no one notices. She works hard to "train up a child" every day and not only does no one notice, but it seems her training is not even having the impact on her child that she would like. There are two hundred pomegranates carved way up in the top of her life where no one sees them, and she wonders, *Do I have any influence at all? If I disappeared tomorrow, would anyone care, or would they just let the trash pile up, get a maid to do their laundry, use paper plates, and order takeout?*

We ask these questions, partly because we are self-centered, but I believe that at the core of these questions what we are really asking is: "God, did you create me for a reason?" and if so, "God, does my life count?"

We want to have an influence on this world and to know that the world is better because God allowed us to be a part of it. The sad part is, we contribute to one another's feelings of invisibility and insecurity. Given our need for acceptance, our battle with pride, and our desire for influence, it is very easy for us to get tunnel vision—to focus only on our own insecurities and to see life from a different view than God's View-Master. We need to allow God to give us peripheral vision.

Basketball players that make it to the big show, the National Basketball Association, have many skills and talents that make them seem almost superhuman. One superhuman ability is the peripheral vision that they possess. It is as if they have the ability to see out the back of their heads. Research has shown that people with this uncanny ability actually have a deep groove in their brain separating the right brain from the left brain, which allows for an extraordinary ability to detect motion and colors. People with this ability can almost sense that something is out of sight.

The guy in front of me at the grocery store definitely did not have this caliber of peripheral vision. It was the Christmas season and he had what looked like a three-week supply of groceries. Every line was packed three and four people back and I was standing behind him with a Diet Coke and a protein bar. I shifted to the left of him waiting for the customary, "Oh, is that all you have? Go right ahead," but he did not see me. I made the classic throat-clearing sound that says, "Hey, I am back here if you want to take a look," and still he did not bite. Finally, after contemplating doing my best song-and-dance routine to draw his attention, I resigned myself to the fact that I was stuck behind a guy who would never make it in the NBA, so at least we had that in common. You know what his problem was? It most likely was not his attitude. I am betting that he would have been the type of guy to let someone with only one or two items move ahead—most people are. It was not that he disliked me; in fact, I am pretty sure he did not even know me, and if he had met me . . . well, that goes without saying. What it all boiled down to was that he had tunnel vision when it came to seeing other people. He just was not looking.

Sometimes my vision stinks. I walk through hallways with my head down deep in thought about all the things that matter to me and disregard the fact that other people exist. I come home thinking about the hard day that I have had or the big game that is on and never notice that the house is sparkling clean, the girls smell sweet, and my favorite food is ready. I am just not looking.

When we start to take a longer, wider view of our world, we can get beyond our own pride and see opportunities to serve others, not just in ways that are immediately appreciated (as my moving forward in the checkout line would have been) but also in ways that no one really notices. These are the opportunities to do things at thirty-four feet in the air, where maybe only God can see. Rather than just slapping on some putty and some paint, these may be the most important moments in our lives. What if it is the culmination of all these small decisions to see beyond ourselves that really matters to God? What if Jesus was completely serious when he said that if we would simply love God with all of our heart (and see from his view) and love others as ourselves (seeing them from his view) that the rest of the law would be a gimme? That would change everything. Making the most of these opportunities will change our perspective, and it may even start to give us some peripheral vision in our lives and connections with others.

It is at this point in our story that Huram seizes an opportunity to get over his own pride and create some barely noticeable works of art, and in so doing shows us his love for God. Huram climbed to the top of that column and carved two hundred pomegranates for an audience of one.

an audience of one

When my little girl Isabelle was about twelve months old she started to really be able to run. Up until that point she had been walking pretty slowly and would occasionally waddle to a speed somewhere close to a jog; but I remember on one day she just took off like a cannonball out of the gun. OK, maybe it was more like a Slinky going downhill, but you get the point. I was amazed and jumped up to follow after her when she gave me "The Look." If you are a parent, you know "The Look" of which I am speaking. It is the over-the-shoulder, back-toward-you look, accompanied by a big grin that says, "Look, Daddy; look, Daddy; look what I am doing." I love that look. It occurred to me on that day, that in that moment and in other moments just like it for a very few more years to come, the only person in the world who Isabelle cared was watching was her daddy. It did not matter that there were other people in the world or what they thought about her running; she wanted me to see. I was an audience of one, and she was doing her best just for me. Read this passage again.

> First he cast two pillars in bronze, each twenty-seven feet tall and eighteen feet in circumference. He then cast two capitals in bronze to set on the pillars; each capital was seven and a half feet high and flared at the top in the shape of a lily. Each capital was dressed with an elaborate filigree of seven braided chains and a double row of two hundred pomegranates, setting the pillars off magnificently. He set the pillars up in the entrance porch to The Temple; the pillar to the south he named Security (Jachin) and the pillar to the north Stability (Boaz). The capitals were in the shape of lilies. (1 Kings 7:15-22)

As you read the details of this passage, some of you may be saying, "Big deal." The first time I read this passage—probably the first one hundred times I read this passage, to be truthful—I never really got the beautiful picture of worship that is happening. I would read about the "bronze pillars, each eighteen cubits high and twelve cubits around" and wonder what this could possibly have to do with anything useful in my life. Then in verse twenty the description of these columns gets even more specific: the filigree; the braids; the pomegranates; the lilies. God, through the writer of 1 Kings, relates the minutia of each and every one of Huram's actions. Why does it matter how intricate these carvings were, and what the exact size of each bowl was, and where the pomegranates were located, and that there were two hundred of them? Our eyes may start to glaze over like they do whenever we get to a section of the Bible with a lot of "begats" in it, but consider that maybe it's not the details themselves that are important, but the fact that they are included in the story in the first place. Why does God give us such details? Because details matter to God.

Several years ago my wife mentioned that she would really like to have a light on our ceiling fan. (I know, this seems to be a recurring problem. I promise, I am in a group to help me kick the habit of trying to be handy.) I think, knowing my giftedness in this area, it was more like a request for me to get someone else to help me install the light, but nonetheless, it was something that she really wanted. We went to the store one night and bought a kit. Unfortunately, simply buying the kit gave me neither the motivation nor the magical superpowers to be able to accomplish the task at hand. So, it sat in our garage for three months before my wife finally just took it back to the store.

Several months after that, I found that six months and the birth of our little girl had not erased this desire from my wife's heart, and this necessitated that we move forward with the project once again. After buying another kit, I mentioned to a friend that I was going to hire someone to come and install it. "Shawn," he lovingly said, "anyone, I mean anyone, can hang a light kit on a ceiling fan. Just read the instructions and it will take you ten minutes max." For some reason that, unfortunately, I cannot blame on drugs or alcohol, I believed him. Because of my friend's well-intended deception, I embarked on the adventure that will be known forever as "the day Shawn almost blew up the house." Just as my friend advised, I got out the instructions, and after weeding through the Spanish version, the French version, the Chinese version, and the Louisianan version I finally found the English version and followed the directions to a T. I was up on the stepladder and got to the point where I was to twist red wires with red wires and black wires with black wires and, unbelievably, it really had been only about ten minutes. My friend was right. I was a hero. I was starting to get thoughts of perhaps giving hardwood floors a shot again. As I twisted the wires together, I felt as if something was missing. I asked my wife if there were more instructions, anything else in the box, anything that had fallen out of the box. I got a "nope," but still, it just seemed weird to leave wires raw like that. Then it dawned on me—tape! We needed tape. I looked around for masking tape, duct tape, or any kind of tape I could find, and in my very nice toolbox I managed to find some Scotch tape. I will give you a minute to gasp. I did not know to gasp. I figured the only thing the tape did was keep the wires together, so why in the world did it matter what color it was? The wires would be tucked away underneath the cover to the fan, thirteen feet in the air. No one was going to see this anyway, so how much could such a minute detail matter? So, I Scotch-taped my wires together, went and turned on the breaker (at least I knew to turn the breaker off before working on the light), and flipped the switch to my new ceiling-fan light.

Have you ever heard the collision of two metal cars? Not the new wimpy fiberglass we have now, but the metal to metal of the late 1970s? That sound happened in my house, but with just a little more of a thud. The lights flickered and then the breaker threw. Because this was not enough fun, I went out and tripped the breaker back on, and it happened again. Being a very curious person, I thought, *Let's give it one more try*, and decided to "rinse and repeat" once more; and a Ford LTD crashed into a Chevy Nova right in my living room for the third time. At this point, the smart one in our family said, "Hey, maybe we should not try that again." So I did what I always do in times of destroying my house. I called my dad, who lives about ten houses down the street. He came over, and when he took the cover off of the fan the smell of burning metal started to waft through our house. As he looked in he saw that the black wires and the red wires that I had twisted together had literally welded themselves to the metal in the fan. Apparently the black tape is called electrical tape for a reason and Scotch tape does not really do the job. Who knew?

Details matter; but because I thought this was something that would never be seen by human eyes, not knowing that it would blow up my house, of course I ignored the details and took care of what I thought mattered—the things people would see.

When we begin to see the direct correlation between the details of our lives and our worship to God, there will be an unbelievable transformation in our lives. When we see that we are performing some of our best work for an audience of one, it will change the way we perform. It will change our lives. Our decisions will look different. We will see people differently and the way we view God, the world, and ourselves will change dramatically.

artist's reflection

Every day we have the opportunity to apply this fourth principle that we see demonstrated in the life of Huram. We encounter opportunities to serve others in ways that only God will see.

: What are some of the actions in your life that you feel go unnoticed by people?

: What are ways that these actions are worship toward God?

: Are there parts of your life that you are intentionally living at seven feet, hoping to be noticed and appreciated by people?

: How can you have a better vision for your life that looks for opportunities to serve without notice?

artist's reflection

cliff cannon

ARTIST PROFILE

A Life Lived at Thirty-four Feet

In Big Daddy Weave's song "Audience of One," it is written in the chorus:

To my audience of one,
You are Father, and you are Son.

People who truly live their lives as unto an audience of one are very hard to find. The first truth is that there just are not many of us who live our lives this way. The temptation is strong, and we often give in to performing for a larger audience in search of our small piece of fame and notoriety. The second truth is that these people's godly view in and of itself makes it difficult to recognize and spotlight the things that they do. In other words, their lives are lived for the most part at thirty-four feet. To truly see these selfless efforts in their lives, it often takes some time getting to know these individuals before you will ever begin to know all that they do at this high altitude. A life lived at thirty-four feet is an accumulation of small details, countless unsung actions, two hundred little pomegranates, and a thousand links of filigree chain—significant in their seeming insignificance.

I am close enough to at least one man who serves an audience of one to have witnessed his high-altitude heroics. Cliff Cannon is my dad. The last name is confusing, I know. To be technical, he is not my father in the biological sense. I actually did not even meet him until I was nine years old, thus the different last name; but he is my dad in every way.

You've read about his attention to detail in home-improvement projects, and the fact that he is an amazing artist and metalworker. (When I picture Huram up on that column, welding rod in hand, he looks just like my dad.) You've also read about how he was willing to jump in, like so many I am grateful for, and help raise me into the man I am today. You see, my mom was an awesome mom, always there for me, and she is one of my best friends even today; yet the one thing she could not be for me was a dad. Cliff Cannon was a man who decided that he would be that dad in my life. He also was the type of man who I saw loving my mom in a way that no man ever had before—and as a twelve-year-old young man I was honored to give the permission that he asked I grant when he wanted to marry my mom. I think my mom may have had something to say about it had I said no, but we did not have to go there because of the type of man Cliff was. My dad has always done everything fully. I was about ten years old when he accepted Christ, and I remember that he placed an ad in the local paper to announce it to everyone. He wanted to make sure everyone knew he had changed. He was a man who was able to model for me what a man who took his responsibilities seriously looked like.

This is all wonderful, of course, and I think that it is worthy of mention, but not many people know the secret that marks him as a man who works for an audience of one: my dad works for God. In 1991, he told me for the first time that he felt a very real calling into ministry and that he felt like God wanted him to be a pastor, whatever that would look like for a welder. He started taking any classes that he could get his hands on. He took seminary classes, read a steady diet of books on ministry, and most importantly, began to serve in his local church. It has been many years since that conversation, and many prayers later my dad's dream of becoming a vocational pastor has not yet come true. What many do not know, and what I often think he does not even realize, is that he is as much pastor as I am in every sense of the word. In fact, it is because of one pastoral action he took that I am who I am today.

When I was in high school I knew that I wanted to go to seminary and become a pastor; but I also wanted to get married to my high-school sweetheart as soon as possible. Those two goals did not seem to go together, so I decided to skip college after one very expensive semester, which my dad paid for, and give it a go as a factory worker in my hometown. My dad never questioned it; he just waited. One day I mentioned that I thought I might have made a mistake. Without hesitation he offered to pay for my school again and encouraged me to go for it. It was his encouragement that helped me complete college in three years so I could indeed marry my sweetheart and then head off to seminary. At one point in my seminary studies he called out of the blue and asked if I needed anything. I told him that I just did not know how I would be able to pay for the next seminary semester and that I would probably need to drop out a semester and just work. A week later I got a small scribbled note from my dad that said, "Remember your debt is cancelled, and so is your seminary bill." I kept that handwritten note in my Bible for many years after the fact. I know these may sound like the things that are ordinary for a dad, and they probably are, but this is a man who *chose* to be my dad. He is a man who chose to do the little things to help me succeed, and he is a man who does it all for an audience of one. He does the things that matter at thirty-four feet. The beauty of it all, as I look back now twenty years later, is that I believe he became my dad because it was the right thing to do, with no guarantee that I would ever notice, or for that matter, even care.

One of the first things that our home church asked my dad to do was to start preaching and organizing the other preachers at a very small church in a rural area that only about fifteen senior citizens attended. There was no fame to be found and certainly no road to advancement—just some pomegranates at thirty-four feet that needed to be crafted. Every Sunday morning, for more than ten years, my dad was faithful to be there to open up that church. If my parents had not moved an hour away from this mission church in order to live closer to my wife and me, and to attend the church that I now have the pleasure of serving, he would still be showing up with the key every Sunday morning.

As a part of his responsibility to that little country church, he also started to print a small bulletin to hand out each weekend. The organist would call him each week with the order of service, and he would carefully type it up with his large, calloused, metalworker hands, and print enough for each person to have one. Just a few months ago he called me over for some wireless connection issues he was having with his PC. (My dad helps me with things that come from Lowe's, and I help him with anything that comes from Dell. I think I got the better end of the deal.) I noticed a stack of papers sitting on his printer. They were the weekend's bulletins. He was still faithfully printing them each week and making sure they got to that little church an hour away. This is thirty-four-feet stuff. My dad is pastoring those fifteen people as a great offering to his audience of one.

The baristas at Starbucks know me by name. Well, by the name "Cliff's son," at least. You see, it's not because I get to speak every now and then for ten thousand people on a weekend; or because I am a local pastor; or because I am handsome, charming, and humble. It's because my dad is a pastor. Every day he goes into Starbucks and talks with the baristas. He knows their names, their life stories, and their children's stories. He talks to them about their college experiences and then comes back again and again. And he always invites them to church. They know that he is going to invite them to church. They also know that he will pray for them, accept them, and even tip them. This is thirty-four-feet stuff. My dad is pastoring those baristas.

One of the greatest pomegranates that anyone can create is to serve people. It is such an honor and a privilege to see my dad selflessly serving each and every weekend as a greeter at our church. His smiling face at the door on Sundays and his leadership to the teams of people at other doors are acts of real worship to his God.

So how do all these little actions, these small daily decisions, really make a difference? One life at a time. My dad is a reminder to each of us that it is the details of life that matter. It is the cups of coffee with friends, the welcoming face to a stranger, and the worker who you can always count on that make a pastor.

The Bible tells us in the book of Ephesians that we are all called to do the work of ministry. In fact, Paul gives pretty explicit direction to the leaders of the church by saying that it is indeed our job as vocational pastors to equip the people of the church to do the work of ministry. As I watch my dad, I see someone who may not carry the title of "Pastor," but who is in every way a spirit-filled minister of the good news of Jesus Christ. He is an artist in the truest sense.

FIVE

finish what you start

I am a natural starter of stuff. I love starting stuff from scratch. The idea of new business models, new ways of doing common things, new initiatives at work, and even new books invigorates me. While writing *200 Pomegranates and an Audience of One*, my first book, it has taken everything within me to not start working on another book idea that I have. Look for that one in stores soon! I digress, but as I said, I love to start things. It is very difficult for us starters (and maybe you know because you are one too) to be "finishers." I even kept us starters in mind while writing this book, and have tried my best to write a short book. I've aimed to write a book that I would be able to finish if I were reading it, rather than just adding it to the pile of three hundred books that I've abandoned about seven-eighths of the way through.

Though everything within me wishes it were not so, one of the characteristics of God is that he finishes what he starts. If we are to be people of significance, we also need to be finishers. I am not suggesting that we should always finish everything; it is not very smart to start bad ideas, but it is even worse to finish bad ideas. There is definitely a time to quit.

some should be quit

I worked as a bag boy at a local grocery store in the town where I grew up. In my hometown of Moncks Corner, South Carolina, this was a rite of passage of sorts. Sixty percent of all southern men have worked in a grocery store at some point in their lives, according to an informal poll I took of my immediate family. Since my grandfather was the butcher at the local grocery store for forty-plus years, that may be a skewed statistic, but you get my point. Because of this family connection I was given some of the really good shifts—like Saturday mornings.

We only made a buck-fifty an hour for bagging groceries, but on a good Saturday morning we could expect to go home with enough quarters in our pockets to make us "bust a sag" before "bustin' a sag" was even cool. One Saturday I was positioned at the checkout station closest to the exit, bagging up some canned goods and taking my time with the bread and eggs to make sure I scored a great tip, when I heard, "Boy, catch him! He is stealing steaks!" It was the manager who was yelling, and I was the "boy" to whom he was yelling. I am not completely sure what went through my fifteen-year-old brain to make me do what I did next (we can blame it on adolescence), but I took off after the steak thief. He was fast and highly motivated, but I was young and in shape, so the race was on. We ran through town, down Main Street, for about a mile and a half. Right when I was expecting some tables set up with little cups of water and some cheering fans, he took a quick left down a side street. Because I was familiar with the route, I knew that street would dead-end at the entrance to an old lumberyard. It was at that moment that I started to feel very manly because I was sure I had caught him. It also started to sink in that I had not really considered what I would *do* when I caught him. I mean, the chase had been fun, but I had not had to physically restrain anyone since . . . well, never. As I rounded the corner, I saw that he'd actually gone into the lumberyard and I had somehow lost him among the stacks of wood. I started jogging slowly around the place when I heard the distinct sound of a large object rushing through the air right by my head. I realized that I had indeed found him. More accurately, he had found me, and he was swinging a two-by-four at me like a four-year-old in his first tee-ball game. I did not like being the ball on top of the tee.

At this point I began to reexamine my idea. As stated earlier, I made about a buck-fifty an hour. The real money, like forty dollars in cold hard cash, was in the tips from little old ladies. On a good Saturday I could bring my hourly wage up to five dollars an hour—that was big time for a fifteen-year-old in Moncks Corner. I quickly noticed that there were no little old ladies in the lumberyard. My suspicions were that the steak thief was not going to tip me. So for this fifteen-minute three-kilometer race I had just run, I was going to be paid around thirty-eight cents. Subtract the cost of stitches and add the pain and suffering of getting whacked on the head by a two-by-four, and this was beginning to look like a bad idea. I remembered at this point that I was young and in shape and that my new friend was highly motivated, so I turned around and ran very fast back to the grocery store. It was a "steal one steak, get two free" Saturday as far as I was concerned. Some ideas are not worth finishing.

It is when we are placed by God in a situation—given the opportunity to be great, to do something, and to invest in others what might only be seen by God—that the greatest story our lives may ever tell of God's greatness is that we finished that great something we started. The only thing worse than finishing a bad idea is not finishing a God idea.

some are worth finishing

In 1995 I married my best friend, high-school sweetheart, and the only girl I had ever dated longer than a month. We were young and in love. Like many young couples, we started our marriage journey with our tanks really low on maturity and experience, just racing downhill on fumes of love. Just like any college student who has driven "one more time" to class on an empty tank knows, eventually even the fumes give out. No one told us year number two was going to be uphill with no fuel stations on the way. In fact, my wife and I would both say that our second year of marriage was the hardest year of our lives. We changed cities and jobs twice in fifteen months, moved four times, and somewhere along the way figured out we were poor and that credit cards have to be paid off. No one ever warned us how hard it would be to "love the one you're with." My wife and I have talked a lot about it over the many years since then and both admit that there were a lot of nights when we wondered if we had made the right choice. I think we both wondered if we should cut and run before we had children, while we were young, and before somebody really got hurt.

It was during these times of questioning that we would reenvision what our lives were to God. We realized that our lives were works of art before a God who intended to finish what he started. Within both of us was a desire to live a life of meaning and influence, and even at twenty-two years old we knew our marriage was one of those ideas that was a God idea and was worth finishing strong. We realized that if we would allow God to chisel where needed, redesign our plans, and paint new colors on the canvas of our hearts that we could get great at this marriage. We could learn together how to do something that mattered, how to invest in each other. We would become less and less selfish as time went on, and in the end, while many of the small gestures and personal sacrifices we made would only be seen by God, that would be OK, because he was our real audience in this great play that we call marriage. We finally caught the vision that our lives, therefore our marriage as well, were acts of worship to God. So we decided—we made a conscious choice and commitment—to finish what we started. We knew that we were not equipped to finish the race, but we decided that we would put our hearts into learning and allowing God to create a masterpiece out of our marriage.

I have heard it said by many a successful person that the facts are many, and many people come up with great ideas every day, but there are very few who have the wherewithal to finish an idea to its completion and make a difference in the world.

It is with this knowledge that the last statement history records about Huram is the statement that tells us the most about his character and which reminds us of how we should live our lives: "So the work on the pillars was finished" (1 Kings 7:22 NLT).

Huram finished what he started. This small statement about a seemingly obscure character in a seemingly irrelevant Old Testament story may be one of the more larger-than-life principles in Scripture. I find it very telling of the character of God that these eight little words were included. It seems that completion is a big theme in Scripture.

God started the idea of perfection in the garden and finished it with Jesus on a cross with the very words, "It is finished."

God promises us that he will finish what he started in us, and he calls it a good work.

God is using you and me, very ordinary people, all over the world to influence the lives of people he loves and to be a part of finishing their story.

God chooses to lift out of the story of building one of the greatest structures in the world the mundane fact that Huram had finished his construction project.

I know this about God: God is a finisher.

Here is what I know about you: Right now there is a work in you that God has not given up on. You may have; but God has not.

You are tired. God is full of energy and fully engaged in your life.

You believe that depression is just a part of who you are, but God already sees it as a part of who you *were*.

You think that your relationship with your spouse is over, and your spouse does too, but God already knows the story of restoration that you will soon tell.

You believe that your children are gone. You have tried your best but now they are running from you and they are running from God, and you know in your heart that it may be over. But God knew about you and your children when he told a parable about a wayward son who came running back to his father. He was thinking about you and he was concerned with you, and he chose to illustrate that concern because he knows how it feels for his wayward children to run back into his arms.

You believe that this illness is the end for you. God knows that what awaits you on the other side of this short life is just the beginning.

You think that your goal in life is to just survive, but God has plans for you that have great meaning and that will change this world for generations to come.

God started something in you and he intends to finish it.

God is at work in finishing what he started and he plans on you being added to his wall as another masterpiece of his work.

What are you considering giving up on? What God idea got you so juiced up a year, two years, or maybe even a decade ago that you have just put on the back burner and allowed yourself to quit? What part of you will the world be missing if you give up now?

motivation for the final sprint

I often wonder if perhaps sometimes we don't realize our role in God's major theatrical production that is the human experience. I wonder if we don't realize that we are not just able to enjoy this life, but that God has asked us to help and create this work with him. And yet, we work so hard and we give up just when we are about to finish. Like a novel without a climax, our lives are left with potential as a final chapter.

It would take much resolve and a passion that can come only from God, but with just one more step we could go down in history as someone who finished well. It would take resolve and passion and looking to a higher purpose, but with one more step, if we could just realize how much God was willing to pay for this great work that he started, we would "SEE" clearly for a change. A friend of mine once told me that often it takes a

Significant **E**motional **E**xperience to trigger this kind of resolve in our lives.

Do you ever have a thought, or maybe a word that you hear, or even a picture or a smell that reminds you of a significant emotional experience that happened in your life? It triggers an emotion within you that reminds you of a better time, a place where you really knew that God was really working in your life. This recollection, many times, can become a moment of worship. Experts say smell has the strongest connection to memory and that a certain aroma can take you back to a significant time or place faster than any other sense. I don't know about you, but for me, it's a song that does it best.

My wife and I started dating in 1991. She was a junior in high school and I was a senior, and Jesus had just recently saved us both when we caught each other's attention. We soon found that in addition to Jesus we had a lot of other things in common, most of all that we both loved music. We collected and critiqued music and related life to music in many ways. With this love of music in common, of course we had to have "our song." We were together in my 1988 Ford EXP one day when we heard the song that really seemed to fit who we were; and the wonderful song "Love That Will Not Let Go" by Steve Camp became "our song." Even to this day I can dial up that song on my iPod and it will send my mind wandering to a place where a seventeen-year-old boy fell in love with a sixteen-year-old girl. It takes me right back to that very day as if it were yesterday, and it also strengthens my resolve for this man to love that girl who has become a woman and a mommy.

We have a picture of my daughter, which is hanging in her room, that I took with my phone's camera when she was about ten seconds old. People say that a picture is worth a thousand words. This picture embodies volumes of a great work of literature that is still being created right before my eyes. Every time I glance at this photo, I am taken back to that day and a significant emotional experience that changed my life forever. I can remember every detail of that moment. I remember my thoughts were frozen in time, and as I gazed into those big, very blue eyes I knew my life would never be the same again. I can bring that very thought into mind even now, and I know that God did something special during those moments.

Songs, pictures, smells—they can transport our minds to this emotional place in an instant. We can find ourselves in a place where something very special was started and it gives us a reason for continuing.

I imagine that day after day as Huram was molding those bronze pomegranates that no one would ever see, he had many moments of doubt and of pondering his purpose. Was there meaning in what he was doing? Was there more? Would he influence anyone? Even the best artists have these thoughts.

In a 2007 interview with *60 Minutes*, football great Tom Brady, who was on the verge of one of the greatest football seasons in NFL history, said this:

> *Why do I have three Super Bowl rings and still think **there's something greater out there for me?** I mean, maybe a lot of people would say, "Hey man, this is what is." I reached my goal, my dream, my life. Me, I think, **"God, it's got to be more than this."** I mean this isn't, this can't be what it's all cracked up to be.*

The reporter asked him if he had any answers. Brady's response:

> ***I wish I knew. I wish I knew**. . . . I love playing football and I love being quarterback for this team. But at the same time, I think there are a lot of other parts about me that **I'm trying to find.** (emphasis added)*

I have had these questions. I imagine you have, too. There are moments when the significance of your efforts is unclear and you are not sure it's worth pressing on. I am pretty sure that Huram had these moments as well. Then, in an instant, because of a thought or because of a smell, Huram was taken back to being a boy who learned lessons from his father of how to leave his mark on life. He was taken back to that moment when Solomon asked him to join in on this great act of worship before him, when he knew that this was a larger-than-life idea. He knew this was something special.

The Apostle Paul seems to have one of these sudden reminiscences as he is writing his letter to the Ephesians from his jail cell in Rome. This memory reminds him of the higher calling he is pursuing, and gives him the strength to press on.

Ephesians 3 (NIV) begins with the words, "For this reason . . ." This first statement gives us all a reminder of what Paul has been saying in the first two chapters of this great letter; and then Paul takes us along with him on a quick little mental trip back in time. He had spent the first part of this letter talking about the fact that we have been separated from God by sin and now we have a great need for a savior. We were all in sin. God adopted us with a price. Jesus paid that price. Because of that adoption we have the opportunity to be a part of God's family. Thinking about "this reason" reminds Paul of the significant emotional experience he'd had years before, when God saved him.

His mind drifts here like a father telling his son a story from his childhood—a story that is deep with both emotion and meaning, but which also serves as a future milestone to the hearer of what could and should be. He takes a few paragraphs of this letter to tell us a little about himself and why he does what he does and what we should be as God's people. This is a great "I digress" moment where Paul loses himself in his thoughts.

It is important to note that God saw fit to include this in Scripture—a brief A.D.D. moment of sorts where we learn about Paul's passion. I think that God chose this because it is a teaching moment for us. It is often in our wandering minds that we discover our true passions, and as we see Paul's passion, we are compelled to examine our own passions. As we hear of Paul's purpose, we must ask ourselves difficult questions that are a little uncomfortable, to make sure that our purpose lines up with that of God's purpose for our lives:

Why was I born?

Why did Jesus choose to save me?

What is it that God has called me to in this world?

Am I willing to make the sacrifices necessary to accomplish that purpose?

These are not easy questions to ask in moments of spiritual self-examination. Sometimes the answers are hard to swallow. Sometimes we have to admit that maybe we do not completely have the answers.

As Paul remembers the moment Christ was revealed to him, he remembers his motivation for finishing strong, which we can learn as well. He emphasizes that his life is a sacrifice. Paul lets us know that even though the Roman emperor Nero may physically hold him, he is there for Jesus, making his life a sacrifice to God in the quiet moments of his heart that only God can see. Paul, in the middle of a Roman jail, was indeed at thirty-four feet.

Finishing what we start will not always be easy. If it were easy, everyone would finish; but Paul reminds us that to live and work for God is to be a sacrifice.

Many in Paul's time, just like today, were misled and thought being a Christ follower meant having an easier life; having all their desires met—even making them rich; or having more time and more energy. But the truth is that following Christ will cost us time, energy, and affections of our heart. We have trained ourselves to believe that if God really wants something to happen, the path will be paved with ease. We often quit something not because it is something that should be quit, but simply because we are not willing to make the sacrifices needed to sustain the race.

Huram had to be willing to be adopted into Solomon's vision and then to truly give up a piece of himself and leave it at the top of the columns.

Huram had to give up a lot of his **time**. Our time is probably our greatest offering to God. Every now and then it's good to think through our week and ask, "Does following Christ affect the decisions I make about what I do with my time?" Are your dreams and the measure of your influence affected by poor use of your time?

Huram had to give all of the **energy** that was left in his life. Huram was most likely an older man, given his reputation and skill. He could have conserved his energy and coasted through life, but instead, he chose to give his second half of life completely to something of worth.

God has given us our energy as a commodity of value. Will we leave it on the table? Will we waste and squander it? Will we use it to create a life of meaning and influence? The decision is ours.

Huram had to be willing to leave behind the **affections** of his heart. There were dreams Huram had for his business and thoughts of fame that had to be given up in order to meet the needs of this project. There were moments he missed at home with his family that were sacrificed for the sake of completing his task well.

If life is to be art, it is often a sacrifice. An artist always leaves a piece of himself or herself with his or her creation.

buddy, you did good

I told you how my grandfather made a decision to invest in my life. His choice was to leave a legacy and to make sure that the legacy finished well. He did not just make a passing decision; he made a lifelong decision that would see my grandmother and him sacrifice much to be there for my mother and myself. He raised me through my childhood into high school, saw me accept Christ and get baptized, saw me meet and marry my beautiful wife, and even sent me off to seminary to train to be a pastor.

When I was twenty-two years old (that horrible second year of marriage), my grandfather, Papa, was coming to the end of a six-month-long battle with very aggressive cancer. He was only sixty-seven years old, but it was obvious that he was not going to win this battle, though we knew he had already won the war.

My wife and I were living in Raleigh at the time while I attended seminary. I had decided earlier that year to delay my graduate education to stay at home with Papa and help take care of him, but he threatened to kick my butt if I let his illness delay my life (and even as a very sick man I knew this former army man could do it), so I went off to start seminary. Even in his illness, he was still teaching me about responsibility and being a man. Connie and I would come down as often as we could to see Papa, each time knowing that we were even closer to it being the last time I would see this man who had chosen to raise me even when it was not the easy choice.

When I bought my first vehicle that Papa was not directly involved in helping me purchase, I sat by his bed to tell him all about my new (well, new to me, anyway) pickup truck. He had a very hoarse throat and was in much pain, so he did not talk much, but he loved to listen to us. He cracked a very slight smile as I told him about the truck. He loved to hear good things about his "buddy." That's what he called me.

As Connie and I were beginning to leave to go back to Raleigh, I leaned in to give him a kiss on the cheek when he pulled me close. As he did, he spoke these words: "Buddy, you did good."

I cannot tell you the impact those four words had on me. Writing them now gives me that same life-stopping significant emotional experience that we saw Paul have earlier. In many ways, despite Papa's illness, that was one of the most encouraging times of my life. All my life, I had been trying to be a man who my Papa would be proud of. He had worked so hard to make sure that I understood character and good choices. He had taught me words like *honor, resolve, work ethic, excellence,* and *family* with very few words and a lot of actions. I took seriously the approval of my Papa, and in four short words he had just given me all the approval I could ever want. Even if I had known those would be the last words I would ever hear from my Papa, I probably could not have imagined them better. God is a great playwright.

I got a phone call the next day telling me that Papa had gone to be with Jesus. I took great joy in those last words. As I knelt in my living room and wept for the loss, I was also struck again by those words and knew that when it came to raising me, Papa knew he had finished well. He had told my grandmother all she meant to him, but he did not have to, as he had showed her with his life. He had pulled his oldest son in close and told him, "Take care of your mother," but he did not have to, because that is the very character he had instilled in his son for thirty years. He let his three girls know that they meant the world to him, but I know they never doubted that. He had lived a life of significance and influence.

I have thought about those words thousands of times over the many years since that day in my grandfather's hospital room. I replay that scene in my mind when I am considering a choice that could forever change my life. Those words have catapulted me to repentance when I have made decisions that were not decisions of character. In my mind, I have traded places with my Papa and imagined one day having that very conversation with my children. I have been influenced by the fact that it was not just approval of me but also a validation of the life of a dying man who simply had wanted to make a difference.

Over the years I have also realized that if that conversation had that much impact on my life, how much more impact will the conversation with Jesus have when he looks at me and says, "Well done, good and faithful servant"? In other words, "Buddy, you did good." I want to finish what I start and I want to finish it well.

A friend of mine and I were talking about our shared interest in running road races, particularly ten-kilometer races. He said he had been very surprised at his final quarter-mile performances in a few races, and in an effort to see what was happening he had asked his wife to videotape him. In his mind he felt that he was running strong, sprinting to the finish with every ounce of his being; but as he watched the video, it told a different story. He said that he watched himself move in an almost comical slow motion as he approached the finish line. Crawling babies were passing him; little old ladies out for a stroll were yelling, "Move it or lose it!" OK, I know I am given to hyperbole, but you get the point. In his mind he was finishing well, but in reality he was in need of correction in order to run the race the way he wanted. He needed to prepare better.

Are you prepared to finish well? Have you gotten great—I mean really great—at something? Have you stopped procrastinating and decided to do something meaningful with your life? Are you investing your time, your energy, and your affections in things that last and benefit others? Are you willing to leave the limelight of the arena floor and climb all the way to the top of the ladder and perform for an audience of one—the only One whose opinion really matters?

God has written a part just for you in the great drama. There is no understudy. You are the only you and the play starts now. Break a leg.

artist's reflection

Every day we have the opportunity to apply this fifth principle that we see through the life of Huram. We see our character Huram walk off the scene with some of the greatest words that could be said about a person: "He finished what he started."

: What are a few words that would symbolize finishing well in your life?

: Make a list of people whose opinion of how you finish matters to you.

: If you were to leave this life today, would you be satisfied with the life you have lived?

: If not, how can you get there?

artist's reflection

A Wife, Mother, and Woman of No Regrets

In school year 1966–1967, Charlene Hornsby was the high-school homecoming queen and a real catch to all who knew her at Baton Rouge High School. At the age of seventeen, she and Billy found themselves in love, and she was pregnant. Billy and Charlene were not following Christ. Billy attended a local Catholic church regularly, but Charlene only came occasionally. They had very little spiritual background and didn't know Christ. They were two young people without faith facing a situation that could have shaken the faith of the faithful. Even through this, however, God was already working in their lives for a future and a plan that he had for them.

Given all of the circumstances, it is surprising that when many people suggested that they "take care" of their situation, these two young people knew they could not do that and, though the timing was not perfect, a family together was all they really wanted. After getting married at seventeen and having another daughter at nineteen, life would find Charlene Hornsby pregnant with her third daughter at the ripe old age of twenty-one years old—the same year that she would celebrate her fourth wedding anniversary. Life had certainly grown up Charlene and Billy quickly.

That year would also begin a journey that has lasted the past thirty-eight years and has been a catalyst for creating one of the best women I have ever met. In 1970, at the age of twenty-one years old, while pregnant, Charlene would learn that she had Hodgkin's disease and would have sixty days to live. For the second time in their young lives it would be suggested that they might want to have an abortion because of this life sentence that Charlene had been given. This news was devastating to the young couple. Over the next few months Charlene would undergo three surgeries and forty-two radiation treatments, and life would be excruciatingly painful. Charlene prayed what she calls a "prayer of desperation" to a God she was not sure even existed. Lying in a bed, unable to move, and presumably at the complete end of her life, she cried, "Lord, if you truly exist, please heal me so I can raise my babies."

Billy likes to interrupt the story here to tell about her wooden dinette set. Charlene had wanted this pine dinette set from a local furniture store. The young couple had no money and had to sleep on the floor of a relative's house during treatments in New Orleans, but this young husband wanted to give his wife the joy of that furniture. So being the industrious man that he still is today, he went down to the furniture store to see if he could have ninety days to pay off the furniture. He reasoned that since Charlene only had sixty days to live he would take the dinette set back after her death and she would get to enjoy it in the time she had left—financial problem solved. Well, as would happen so many more times in her life, Charlene's prayer was answered—and Billy had to pay for that dinette set.

Billy arrived home one day after leaving his wife in what he can only call "the last days of her life" to find her having cleaned the house, hung the laundry, and begun working on the dishes. Charlene says she was just tired of everyone else having to do her work. God heard her prayer. Six years later Billy and Charlene would both commit their lives to Christ and the story would continue. Over the next thirty-four years, Charlene would face reoccurring bouts with raging fevers, residual sickness from the radiation, skin cancer, chronic leukemia, and other cancer diseases that would seem to beat at her body. Anyone who knows her would say that she seems to have never been sick a day in her life. She had asked to raise her babies, and while she was raising them she did not have time to worry about being sick.

Then in 2007, after such a long journey, yet another opportunity came into Charlene and Billy's life. The cancer is back again and she has been given eighteen months to live. A story thirty-eight years in the making adds another chapter.

While writing and thinking about Huram and his drive to finish well, I realized something about finishing. It has absolutely nothing to do with death. In fact, when you die, how you die, and even how old you are when you die has zero effect on finishing well. It is how you live that counts.

I had a chance to sit down with my friends and ask them a few things about their lives. When Charlene got the news that this may very well be the final chapter in this great saga that has been a great life, she had many opportunities to be fearful (wouldn't we all?), to be bitter (haven't we all?), or to blow it (don't so many?). But instead, when you talk to her, you get the keen understanding that this is someone who is ready to die because she spent a lifetime living.

Asked what she wants to do with the last few months of her life, Charlene smiles and says, "Exactly what I am doing now." She explains that she loves her friends, her family, and her life, and that she has been living her entire life as if tomorrow may not come. She has lived a life that was purposeful and meaningful and full of influence. She has lived a life of "no regrets." Hers is a life that she can look back on and know that she has been faithful to her husband, faithful to her children, and now faithful to her grandchildren. In all of these things, she has been faithful to her God. There are no skeletons in the closet, nothing to hide from or run away from, and nothing that will disappoint the ones she loves. She is ready to walk away, when God pleases, from her canvas, knowing that God will add the final strokes to a masterpiece. Billy says that their life, in many ways, can be summed up in Romans 5:3-5 (NIV): "We also rejoice in our sufferings, because we know that suffering produces perseverance; perseverance, character; and character, hope. And hope does not disappoint us, because God has poured out his love into our hearts by the Holy Spirit, whom he has given us."

It is within this verse that you can sum up four characteristics of someone like Charlene Hornsby, a person who finishes well.

1. Rejoice in Suffering. Charlene says that God has allowed her so much. He has showered her with his grace of salvation and even allowed her to raise her babies and her grandbabies. She has been asked if she thinks about heaven much and her answer is a surprising "No." She says that she has much to do here for as long as God allows her to stay, and that even in this suffering, she has been showered with his grace. She rejoices even in her suffering.

2. Perseverance. Billy describes their life as a life of giving God the time to work things out. This is the practice of waiting for God, being patient with God. With three life sentences of cancer, two pregnancies she was encouraged to end, financial destruction from all of the debt of medical expenses, and seemingly no light at the end of the tunnel, Charlene has persevered. She has waited for God rather than trying to be God. In doing this, she now finds herself with three beautiful children; financial freedom after a life of hard work and paying off what she and Billy owed; and most of all, a life of no regrets because she waited for God.

3. Character. Charlene has been shaped into a woman of strength and beauty and has fulfilled her purpose in an artistic manner. Billy cannot help getting choked up when I talk to him about Charlene. You can tell that he both loves her and respects her like a husband should. She is a woman who he says is completely transparent and open for all to see, with no fakeness to her. Her character shines through as a testimony to Jesus. Charlene says that she always figured she might be the only encounter with Jesus that her children or others would ever have, and she knew she needed to shine.

4. Hope. Time after time God has strengthened the hope that is within this couple. When there was not hope, God was Hope. Charlene puts it plainly like this, "My life can be wrapped up into this statement, 'God is faithful and his Grace is sufficient.'"

Charlene Hornsby has truly practiced the entirety of this book in her life. She has been a great wife and mother; she has always been faithful to do what she was called to do; she has invested in people; and she has done the small things in life that were truly for an audience of one. In doing this, she has had a life of meaning and influence that surpasses all of the influence of all the kings in the world. But most importantly, she has lived in such a way that she is ready to finish what she started. Lord, I pray that it could be said of each of us that we finished well.

Everyone longs to live a life of meaning and purpose, to leave something of real worth behind when they're gone. All too often, we feel that our day-to-day tasks make no difference in the great scheme of things. The truth is exactly the opposite—God has given each of us extraordinary power to create beauty and transform the world through our daily work and ordinary actions. You have immense potential to develop your God-given talents and contribute something that makes a difference in the world, whether it is through construction or counseling, doing people's taxes carefully and ethically, or raising and teaching children. Even if your contribution seems to go unnoticed by others, you can rest assured that God sees and values your work.

You too are an artist, equipped with a palette of skills and strengths that can honor God and influence the world in amazing ways. Where will you make your mark? I pray that God will use you to do something that will create a legacy, and that when he does you will do it as unto an audience of one.

AN ARTIST'S PRAYER

God, I pray that you would remind me that you created me for a life of meaning and influence, ultimately to bring you fame.

I pray that you would continue this work in me and hone my skills, talents, and spiritual gifts in such a way that you would be honored by my greatness.

As I walk in this journey, God, I pray that you would show me what to do, teaching me what the passion of my life should be. Along that journey, I pray that you would allow me to have the courage and the integrity to do something meaningful with my life.

Lord, teach me to see the needs of others as you see them, and to invest in your other people your prized possessions. When I do this, I pray that it would be a beacon that shines on you.

God, as I do these things I pray that you would be my audience. That my love and adoration would be for you and that you alone would get my praise.

And lastly, God, allow me the grace to finish the race well. I look forward to seeing you and hearing you say, "Well done." Lord, give me your strength to finish strong in Jesus' name. Amen.

my artist's reflection

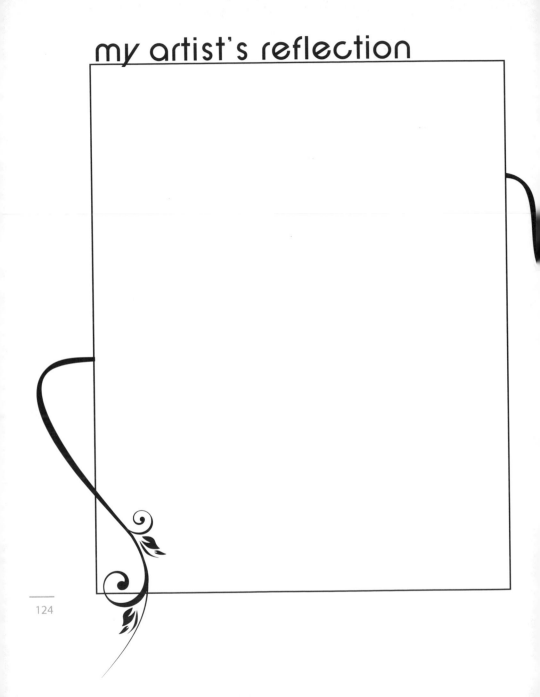

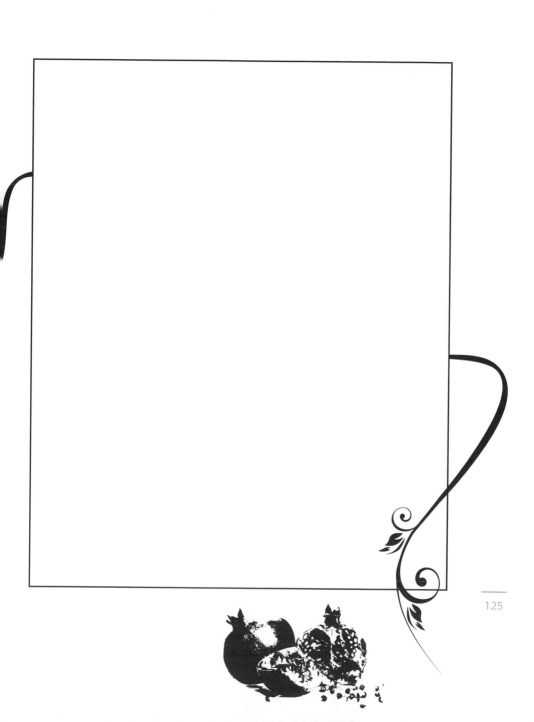